The House on Mary Street –

The Early Years

By:

Dr. Kathryn Hartz Beard

This book is an Ethnographic Oral History of
The Neighborhood Center, Inc.
Located in Utica, New York.
Photos provided by Marie Russo

Copyright © 2012 by Dr. Kathryn H. Beard
All rights reserved

No part of this book may be reproduced in any form or by any electronic or mechanical means including information storage and retrieval systems, without permission in writing from the author. The only exception is by a reviewer, who may quote short excerpts in a review.

Printed in the United States of America

First Printing: November, 2012
ISBN- 978-1-300-37144-1

DEDICATION:

TO:

Madison – for digging though dusty old boxes, sorting papers, helping with copies and cheering me on

Dale – for patience, encouragement, being a sounding board, living with the clutter and my procrastination

Alice – for faithfully serving as a board member of the Center for many years, and encouraging we children to participate, grow, and learn from the programs offered at the Center; and for being the best and most remarkable mother in the world

Betty & Mary – for support, patience, care, spell and fact checking, and encouragement; for taking me to the playground, my first "Blue Bird" meeting, and other activities at the Center

Richard – for the leadership you gave the Center; and for sharing so many experiences at the Center with me

Marie – for the years of service you have given to the Neighborhood Center; for opening your heart and sharing your memories with me; for the support you have given to all members of my family

United Methodist Church – for the vision and support you have given to the Center so that dreams could be realized

CHAPTER TITLES

1. Introduction
2. Settlement Houses
3. Conducting the Research
4. Italian Immigrants to Utica, New
5. The Origins of the Italian Settlement House
6. Deaconess Hattie E. Davis
7. Early Leadership and Programs
8. Miss Helen Marie Edick
9. Miss Ruth Wright
10. The Neighborhood Center
11. Miss Marie Russo
12. Moving Forward
13. An Oral History – Marie Russo
14. Narrative One: Marie Russo's perception of her early life in Utica, New York
15. Narrative Two: Marie Russo's perception of her early experiences at the Settlement
16. Narrative Three: Marie Russo perception of public education during her youth
17. Narrative Four: Marie Russo's perception of the early history of the Settlement
18. Narrative Five: Marie Russo's perceptions of key settlement staff that she feels were influential in her life
19. Narrative Six: Marie Russo's perception of the importance of the Italian Settlement House
20. My Utica
21. My Center

CHAPTER ONE
INTRODUCTION

I believe that there are two things most people need or want; the first, a role model, the latter, a legacy.

When I heard the news that she might soon be gone, it made me pause, because I am part of her legacy. I had not seen her, or frankly thought much about her for some time. I used to send gifts at the holidays, or an occasional check when I was puffed up with a sense of benevolence. They became less frequent as the reality of mortgage payments, groceries, gasoline costs, and the need to fulfill my own wants, to make my life more easy and comfortable, pushed her back into a dimly lit, rarely visited chamber in my brain. I am embarrassed to say, the gifts eventually stopped completely.

It is only when our personal nostalgia arouses a need or longing within us that we once again return to that cavity to revisit the faded images of people, places and events, some happy, some sad, that shaped our personal quest.

I didn't need her anymore. My life was full with family, work, friends and all those other elements that give a sense of success and well-being. This news however, sparked the light in my darkened chamber and I could feel the electricity dance across the tiny wires of the Tungsten filament that lit its walls. I had to see her.

Since I was *home* for a visit, I resolved to drive over that afternoon. I had not been on those streets in over twenty years, not since my mother had sold our family home and moved to the suburbs. All the people I knew then were gone. I drove past the railroad station on Broad and up John Street. I passed St. John's Catholic Church. I smiled as I recalled visits with some of my childhood friends to its grotto, located in the church's basement. Often, during our "tween" years, we would stop there as we ventured past her on our way to the *Boston Store* or other shops and boutiques that once dotted our city, before shopping malls obliterated our downtown.

I wasn't Catholic, although I lived in a predominately Catholic neighborhood. I never told my mother about our visits, perhaps out of some fear that I might get in trouble. Our church did not have beautiful statues and I was enchanted by the ornately decorated shrines. We would descend the street entrance trying to look and act as piously as possible. The nuns in their long robes intimidated me, and I remember wondering what would happen if they found out a Protestant had trespassed into their urban garden.

I have to digress here for just a moment. Let this be my restitution for my many acts of trespassing at this Shrine. It was simply, a beautiful place. I marveled that in a neighborhood often labeled "poor" or "disadvantaged" that the door to this refuge was never locked. It was quiet, it was clean, and it was peaceful.

Above the altar at our church was a stained glass rendering of Christ praying in the Garden of Gethsemane. In St. John's grotto there were three dimensional, life size interpretations that brought the Gospel story to life for me. I wondered if the image I recalled of Christ in a bright red robe talking to an angel was painted in reality or colored by the warm memories it produced as I drove by.

I remember too, the strong presence of women through the shrines in the grotto. I don't remember who they all were, or even why they were considered Saints, but I recall statues of St. Anne and St. Teresa. Around each shrine was a half moon shaped railing with a kneeling pad and Votive candle holders. We always felt obligated to pray, and since I wasn't sure if the Catholics prayed the same way we Methodists did, I decided not to take any chances and would instead recite a prayer that was near the statue of St. Teresa. I chose to kneel at her shrine because my oldest brother's wife was Catholic, and was named Theresa, so I felt it was a safer place for me to pray. I don't remember the prayer, except for one part, "...*In Me and Through Me*..." The words lingered in my thoughts as I continued to drive up John Street.

What gifts do I have *in me* that I have never put to use, and what change for the better might have occurred *through me* if I had used those gifts? Of course, we sprinkled our heads with Holy Water and lit a candle before we left. Occasionally we would drop a dime into the collection box.

Jweid's was the corner store on the block where I grew up. I noticed that it appeared to still be open; however I turned the corner too quickly to see if the name had changed. The large display windows were now filled in with sheets of plywood and the front door had more locks.

I drove down Blandina Street towards my childhood home. The neighborhood houses where I once played were now empty lots. Our home was still there and the familiar red brick called to me. Rising crime rates and years of unfilled promises of "urban renewal" and "neighborhood revitalization," finally convinced our mother to leave. I was married by then and all of my siblings had moved on to other neighborhoods or communities. I never had regrets about leaving, yet it saddened me to see the disrepair the house had fallen into.

The large front porch where we posed for so many Easter photos was gone. It was replaced by a tiny stoop of cement steps reaching up to the front door. There was no hint of the garden my mother had tenderly cultivated. Gone, too, were the ornate bay windows that once decorated the front of our home. I glanced at my former bedroom window. It was open, no screen, and I could see something draped over the sill, half in the room, half resting on the fire escape. I didn't linger.

I continued down Blandina to Mohawk, turned left on Mary and then I saw her. The house on Mary Street. The house that is a legacy to all the women that built her, and dedicated so much of their lives to her.

Edick, Hunt, Wilson, Wright, Russo, Hightower…, I wondered if they knew how many people they had touched and encouraged. The house that forged a spirit of community, within an urban ghetto. The house that taught me skills, and surrounded me with love and friendship. The house that holds so many of my childhood memories, and those memories of thousands of others. The house that built me.

I am part of the legacy of the Neighborhood Center, Inc., located in Utica, New York. A legacy that began with the origins of the Italian Settlement House, as it was initially called. I am part of the legacy conceived through the dedication, sacrifice and tenacity of the women that shaped her, and breathed life into her. The individuals that worked to make the Center meet the needs of the neighborhood it served. They were the role models that helped me to realize my own significance.

A legacy that one day soon might be gone. The passage of time, the shifting of her foundation, and the high costs of repairs, leaves little hope that this edifice to our community will endure a second century. What will endure are the memories and achievements of the thousands of individuals touched by her.

I want to leave a legacy to my children. It might be a simple thing like my great-grandmother's vase. It might be the net worth of the material items that I have accumulated during my working years. It might just be what they remember about me, good or bad. The *in me and through me* acts of kindness or accomplishments I have achieved.

Like many, I am the past, the present and the future of the Neighborhood Center. In me lies the fruition of those that dreamed and believed in the possibilities of the urban poor and through me I will try to preserve the significance of the house on Mary Street. To do so, I will share my memories of the Center and my childhood neighborhood. I will present a historical overview of the early roots of the Center, and I will share the oral history of one of its most significant leaders, and one of my role models, Marie Russo.

615 Mary Street

CHAPTER TWO
SETTLEMENT HOUSES

Settlement Houses began to appear in the late 19th and early 20th century in large urban areas during the industrial revolution. They were organized to help immigrants coming to America more readily assimilate into their new communities. The earliest settlements were located in major metropolitan areas like Chicago and New York City.

Much has been written about Chicago's *Hull House* and its director, Jane Addams. Likewise, Lillian Wald shared her leadership experiences about the *Henry Street Settlement* in New York City. By the early 1900's about 100 settlements had appeared on the East Coast. The *Italian Settlement* in Utica, New York, was one of those original hundred. Comparisons can be made among the social, cultural, and economic needs of the disadvantaged population served by the *Italian Settlement* with settlements found in larger cities.

Many of the early settlements were established to specifically meet the needs of the immigrants and refugees that were pouring into the northeastern cities and trickling west and southward. As women in the early 1900's pushed for the right to prove themselves as capable and independent community leaders, they began to take the leadership in education and social reform (Nettleship, 1982).

Many of the settlement houses were supported through church groups or other special interest groups. *The King's Daughters* organization was a Protestant group that assisted with the development of the settlement house movement. The group was organized in 1889 by Margaret Bottome, the wife of a New York Methodist minister (Buck, 2006). As chapters of the *King's Daughters* developed among Methodist and other Protestant church women, more assistance was given to the increasing number of settlement houses.

The men and women of the American settlement movement were the precursors of the Progressive Movement (1890-1920) and were influenced by the Progressive-era response to urban social problems. It is estimated that 90 percent of early settlement workers were college graduates (Carson, 1990). The Progressive Movement in the United States addressed problems that were caused by rapid industrialization, advances in technology, and the arrival of thousands of immigrants, which combined, altered the social and economic lives of Americans (Axinn and Levin, 1997; Barbuto, 1999).

Settlement houses were catalysts for change within the educational system. The settlements offered classes in English, Civics and basic American History. Early fine arts and vocational curricula in public schools today can be traced to the leadership settlement programs provided in these areas. These programs were a natural extension of the settlements' philosophy of cultural inclusion.

Vocational programs offered at settlements were an integral part of the history of career and technical education (CTE) and were significant in shaping legislation that would emerge to develop CTE curricula in our public schools. This legislation would not have been possible without the efforts of educational reformers like those that were part of the settlement movement (Lannie, 1967; Virginia Cooperative Extension, 2004). Political activism on behalf of vocational education in the late 1890's and early 1900's continued to move the educational reform movement forward. President Theodore Roosevelt, in support of vocational education, believed that if America was to be a contender in world markets that the nation would have to develop the skills needed to compete with nations that already had highly developed business acumen.

Roosevelt is reported to have criticized the public school system for its inability to provide industrial training, including basic tradesmen skills for mechanics, foundry workers and carpenters (Schlesinger, 1957). As the United States competes today with global markets, similar concerns are often echoed in our current educational arena.

CHAPTER THREE
CONDUCTING THE RESEARCH

The *Italian Settlement*, later to be known as *The Neighborhood Center* was under the leadership of Ms. Marie Russo when I participated in the programs and activities of the agency. I am fortunate that I can provide some of "Miss Marie's" memories of her seventy year relationship with the Center. This provides a perspective of the agency's oral history that can be preserved while first-hand knowledge is still attainable. The details of this history cannot be as thoroughly obtained from other known sources.

Marie Russo's unique story with the agency cannot be duplicated. She came to the Settlement as the young child of an immigrant father. Through the support of the Settlement she attended college, worked full time with the Settlement through all of her adult years and ultimately became the agency's executive director.

While there are books written about other settlements, most are done though the eyes of the settlement workers. There are a few brief accounts from settlement participants, but there are no accounts by an individual who grew up receiving the services of the settlement and who then evolved into the primary leadership role of the agency. Preserving Marie Russo's oral history is essential in preserving the history of the Neighborhood Center. There is no other source that can offer the same perspective.

Marie is outgoing and radiates energy and enthusiasm. She is an articulate communicator and her many years of public speaking are evident in the detailed and rich descriptions she used as she shared her perceptions of how the Settlement shaped and influenced her life, and the community in which she lived. The relationship of Marie with the Settlement are so interwoven that I believe that the history of the Settlement cannot adequately be recorded without including the oral history of Miss Russo.

When I began my research, there appeared to be no systematic studies that recorded the early history or the experiences of individuals who used the services of the *Italian Settlement House* except for a brief summary that had been prepared by Ms. Russo and her co-worker, Mary Hightower. A one page summary was also included in a brochure given to me by the agency's director. Documentation for this study was obtained over a three-year period.

My research included field work to obtain, review and evaluate the written historical documents of the Settlement. I used many sources to produce a rich and comprehensive description of the development of the settlement and its influence in the neighborhood. To complete this study, I conducted interviews with key staff and board members. Additionally, I reviewed photographs, journals, historical letters, scrap books, newsletters, written testimonies, newspaper articles, reports and documents.

My research was conducted in different phases. The first phase focused on the collection of historical data on the settlement representing programs and initiatives during the pre- and post- Smith-Hughes legislation era. The second phase addressed the relationship of the settlement with Miss Russo.

Literature reviewed about the Italian Settlement House was obtained from the historical files of the Neighborhood Center, Inc., the Utica Observer-Dispatch newspaper, the Utica Public Library and the Oneida County Historical Society. Historical records relating to the origins of the Settlement House were also secured from the historical archives of the North-Central Conference of the United Methodist Church. There were few documents preserved. The documents that were obtained verified or supplemented information found during the naturalistic inquiry. They added depth and additional dimension to the oral history, annual reports and written accounts about the settlement.

Discussion and review of the historical data was also checked for accuracy with Marie Russo and key staff, including Mary Hightower, Richard Hartz, and Mary Hartz. Current and former board members Betty Youmans, and Alice Nichols were also consulted.

Over the past century, the name of the agency has changed to reflect the diversity of the neighborhood it serves. In the early 1900's, the agency was known as *The Italian Settlement House*. Mid-century, the agency was renamed the *Neighborhood Center*. For this history, "Italian Settlement," "Italian Mission," "Italian Christian Settlement," "Neighborhood Center," "Neighborhood Center, Inc.," and "Center" all reflect the same agency.

In presenting this history, I feel I have a unique prospective. I grew up in the neighborhood served by the agency and participated in many of the activities at the Center. In addition, I worked at the agency while in high school and in college. I have had a fifty year relationship with the Center and Miss Russo who served as the Executive Director when I attended the Center as a child and when I was employed there.

I was familiar with many of the businesses, ethnic pockets, and individuals referred to by Miss Russo during the oral histories. My relationship with Marie served to create a bond of mutual respect allowing for candid conversations between us. It also allowed me the opportunity to examine and obtain copies of photographs and records that would most likely not be available to a researcher who did not have this rapport and relationship. Because of the previous relationship with the agency, I was able to obtain approval to research materials and historical documents stored at the Center.

To further substantiate the validity of this history, significant research of the historic overview of the settlement house movement in America was conducted. Special attention was given to the Italian immigrants who populated New York. Resources at Syracuse University, the University of Virginia, and Virginia Polytechnic Institute (Virginia Tech) were utilized. This included on-site visits to each university.

Resources at Syracuse University were used to help locate demographic information about Utica and the central New York region. Syracuse is located approximately fifty miles from Utica and houses a number of regionally-specific documents.

Virginia Tech, a land-grant college, had extensive resources regarding the importance of settlement houses and the early aspects of their significance in career and technical education (CTE). Many settlements offered programs in home economics, early childhood education, as well as trades classes, such as masonry, carpentry and other CTE related curricula.

Research for this study was conducted as part of my doctoral dissertation with the University of Virginia (Beard, 2010).

CHAPTER FOUR
ITALIAN IMMIGRANTS TO UTICA, NEW YORK

To understand the influence of the Italian Settlement House on the life of Marie Russo and the individuals it served, it is important to examine the impetus that brought Italian immigrants to Utica, New York.

In the United States, between 1869 and 1877, over 29,000 miles of railroad lines were built (Lynch, 2005). By the early 1900's, Utica became a major railroad hub and accommodated a large network of railroads that transported goods throughout the country (Ernst, 1965). With the more advanced railroad systems that sped the flow of materials, the need for skilled workers increased. The Erie Canal and the railroads easily connected Utica to other cities allowing trade from the Great Lakes regions to expand through Utica into Albany, and down the Hudson River to New York City (Ernst, 1965).

Utica was becoming a major manufacturing community in New York State (Crisafulli, 1977). The immigrants were able to find employment in Utica's factories and foundries. Places of worship were established. Many of the immigrants, especially those that did not speak English, chose to maintain their native culture. They used traditional foods, music, and celebrations to segregate themselves and their children from American influences. Immigrants who did not speak English turned to others of their own nationality to help as interpreters.

Some of the immigrants, while highly trained or skilled in their native land, were forced to work as semi-skilled or unskilled laborers because of language barriers or prejudicial attitudes. Some worked as domestic servants to the wealthy that lived in the fine homes and mansions on Rutger and upper Genesee Street (Schiro, 1975).

Important industries in the Utica area included metal and machinery factories. The main source of employment for Italian women in Utica was factory work in the textile industry. The Utica Knitting Company and the Oneita Knitting Mills provided goods and services for consumers worldwide. In 1910, Utica's seventy-two manufacturing companies employed over 18,000 workers. Consumer goods that were manufactured in the Utica area included sheets and pillowcases, knit fabric, swimsuits, sweaters, stockings, hats, and gloves. Goods manufactured included guns, radiators, tools, steam engines, and boilers.

In 1914, one of the largest depots in the New York Central Railroad was built in Utica, employing over 6,000 individuals, many of whom were unskilled Italians immigrants (Crisafulli, 1977; Glazer and Moynihan, 1970). Additionally, there was a large railroad roundhouse and repair shop to support the growing railroad industry (Crisafulli, 1977).

Agriculture around Oneida County was an important economic industry. The Utica area had nearby farms and agricultural businesses that attracted immigrants who had come from rural parts of Italy. Displaced from the farm life they had been accustomed to, Utica provided these immigrants with a sharp contrast to the densely populated neighborhoods of New York City. Many immigrants worked as day laborers on local farms during the harvesting months.

Two major universities in the area had outstanding agricultural programs. Cornell University was founded during the late 1800's as a land-grant college. In 1911, Syracuse University opened its State College of Forestry. In 1912, the Oneida County Farm Bureau and the 4-H Club Association were formed (Crisafulli, 1977). The establishment of these services, prior to the 1914 Smith-Lever Act that provided for a program of cooperative education in agriculture and home economics, further demonstrated the importance of agriculture in the area (Gordon, 2008).

By 1919, over 22,000 immigrants were employed in the Utica area (Crisafulli, 1977). Readily available employment opportunities in construction for the men, and clothing manufacturing plants for the women, made Utica an attractive community for the immigrants. While these manufacturing industries brought large numbers of immigrants to the Utica area in the early 1900's, the decline of manufacturing in Utica eventually led to an economic downturn. Post World War I manufacturing declines, the Depression of the 1930's, and factories relocating to Southern states all contributed to Utica's decline from being an industrial leader. This pushed the Italian community deeper into poverty (Crisafulli, 1977).

In the 1930's, the Italian immigrants, along with their 20,000 children and grandchildren, accounted for twenty-five percent of the city's population. Through the 1970's, Italians would represent the largest ethnic group in the community (Pula, 2005). Shops were opened that catered to specific ethnic groups.

For the Italians, Bleecker Street was an essential trading area. Local newspapers like *Il Pensiero Italiano* and *Il Messagiero Del Ordine* were published for the Italian-speaking residents of the city. The strong work ethic of many first-generation Italian-Americans led them to open many businesses. This was accomplished through the hard work and the expected support of all family members. Business enterprises included family operated stores, restaurants, and wholesale food concerns.

Music groups were formed for many of the immigrant groups. The German population formed the *Maennerchor*, and the *Red Band* was a popular Italian group. These groups were formed to preserve the music and dance of their cultures. They played at local festivals, funerals and dedications.

Immigrant women learning English at the Settlement House

CHAPTER FIVE
THE ORIGINS OF THE ITALIAN SETTLEMENT HOUSE

The *Italian Settlement House* in Utica, New York, was founded in 1905 by the *Women's Home Missionary Society* of the Methodist Church. Protestant churches recognized the need for settlement houses and saw the opportunity to convert some of the new immigrants to their branch of Christianity. Evangelism was one of the goals of the Methodist church, and part of the impetus to establish the *Italian Settlement House.*

The aim of this chapter is to provide an historical framework for the agency. This has been a challenge, as there appears to have been little organization of historical records over the past one hundred years. For this research, boxes of assorted newspaper clippings, scrapbooks, pages from programs, various annual reports, minutes from meetings, letters to and from various staff members, and ledger books were pieced together. Many of these items had initially been prepared by volunteers, often without the date of publication or author's name. Care has been given to create a time line, using multiple sources of verification, as accurately as possible.

Reports were presented each year by district secretaries to the Methodist Church at large, during their yearly Annual Conference. The Northern New York Conference (NNYC) of the Methodist Church initially oversaw the *Italian Settlement House.* The literature available concerning the formation of the agency is found in those parts of the church conference's annual reports that relate to the Settlement.

Rev. J. B. Hammond, Presiding Elder of the Utica District, wrote the first of these annual reports that included information about the Settlement. In 1905, his report to the Northern New York Conference identified the initial location of the Settlement as occupying six rooms of a small two-story building located at 98 Third Avenue in Utica, New York. The facility was referred to as the *Italian Christian Settlement House.* The initial services of the program were provided by a group of volunteer Methodist women who saw a need in East Utica to assist immigrants in filling out naturalization papers. The volunteer workers used the small six rooms to provide basic services and religious programs to the Italians in the neighborhood (Williams, 1980). There is no documentation that suggests that the volunteers lived at the Third Avenue location.

Supporting Hammond's report is a reflective paper by R. E. Meeker written in 1969 and titled, *Six Decades of Service*. The paper reflects on the various mission services of the Women's Home Missionary Society of the Mohawk District between 1880 and 1940, and includes some information on the work at the Italian Settlement (Meeker, 1969).

Meeker discussed the influx of immigrants that swept into the industrial cities in the eastern part of the United States. She noted that mission work among the Italians in Utica was organized, and that Methodist women began a neighborhood service in November, 1905. According to Meeker, two workers were employed (Meeker, 1969). It is reasonable to believe that one was Deaconess Davis, the first director of the settlement

In 2004, Gilbert T. Smith, Chairperson for the Conference Committee on Archives and History of the North Central New York Conference of the United Methodist Church, prepared a report titled, *Historical Review*. This report outlined some of the activities and events that had occurred in the Northern New York Conference. Included in the paper is information about a committee that was formed in 1905 that included the following churchwomen; Mrs. A. Bramley, Mrs. George O. Pennock, and Mrs. I. L. Hunt. This committee met with Bishop Goodsell from the NNYC. The purpose of the meeting was to obtain his consent to organize settlement work among the Italians in Utica. This was to be conducted under the auspices of the Woman's Home Missionary Society of the NNYC (Smith, 2004).

The Methodist Church is a connectional church, in that it is a network of churches with a defined governing structure. Bishops oversee conferences; the conferences are comprised of districts, and district superintendents oversee local churches. Every conference holds an annual meeting at which information about the missions of the Church is shared. Because of this network within the church structure, the Methodist women who helped to organize the Italian Settlement may well have been familiar with the endeavors and efforts of Margaret Bottome, the wife of a New York City Methodist minister, and the King's Daughters organization that she founded in 1889.

A chapter of the King's Daughters was part of the Settlement's programs. Records from the Italian Settlement House clearly identify meetings and projects by their group. As members of the Women's Home Missionary Society, part of the connectional services of the Methodist church, it would be reasonable that they would know about the work of the Methodist women who supported the *Henry Street Settlement* in New York City.

Alice Hunt, who has been credited with being the true catalyst in the early success of the Italian Settlement, was married to a Methodist minister, Rev. I. L. Hunt. Bishop Goodsell would have known about the King's Daughters organization. It is reasonable to believe that Methodist programs serving the immigrants who lived in New York City would have been looked to as models by the women of the NNYC. The fact that the Italian Settlement House immediately organized a Kindergarten program like ones provided at established settlements, also lends support to this idea.

A local board of directors for the new Settlement was organized. The board included: Mrs. Hunt, Mrs. Pennock, Mrs. M. E. L. Dunbar, Mrs. C.D. Rosenkrans, Mrs. Erick Peterson, Mrs. W. L. McIntosh, and Mrs. A. Skinner (Smith, 2004).

Third Street Location. Deaconess Davis is believed to be on front porch

CHAPTER SIX
DEACONESS HATTIE E. DAVIS

Under Bishop Goodsell, in 1906, the NNYC annual report officially recognized the *Italian Settlement* as one of its mission projects and appointed Deaconess Hattie E. Davis to be the first superintendent of the Italian Settlement. As the program grew, so did the need for expanded facilities. Building plans were made to secure a permanent location for the Settlement House. In the meantime, larger, temporary quarters, including living space for Deaconess Davis, were used at 139 Elizabeth Street (Meeker, 1969). Working with Miss Davis was a small staff of three, all believed to be volunteers (Meeker, 1969; Smith, 2004). Funds were obtained to secure the lot at 615 Mary Street as the building site of the permanent *Italian Settlement House*. The Northern New York Women's Home Missionary Society (WHMS) purchased an additional lot giving the Settlement a sizable campus (Smith, 2004).

The 1907 report to the NNYC, submitted by W. D. Marsh, Chairman, and C. E. Miller, Secretary, demonstrated a higher level of awareness of the growing number of Italian immigrants entering the Mohawk Valley and recommended to the Northern New York Annual Conference the formation of a church for the immigrants at the Settlement. Miss Davis cooperated with the conference's decision, and the Italian Methodist Church, that had been organized in 1907, used the Settlement for Sunday morning services conducted by Rev. Valentine Ambrosine (Marsh, 1907).

In 1908, a report delivered to the Methodist Annual Conference discussed the continued growth in the evangelical efforts of the church with the Italian population. It was reported that religious services for the Italians were being held, and that some Italians had accepted the Protestant Christian faith. Funds were sought to assist with the cost of building the permanent Settlement House. The Treasurer's Report showed donations from churches in the NNYC of $1,163.75 for the Italian Mission (NNYC, 1908).

The 1909 report by Rev. Hammond, Mohawk District Superintendent for the NNYC, noted that the work of the Italian Church of Utica had been carried on by a missionary, Rev. Valentine Ambrosine, and a helper. The helper, Miss Ruth Tapping, had attended a women's seminary college, and had prior similar work experience in New York City (NNYC, 1909). Rev. Hammond's 1910 report, noted the purchase of an additional lot for the Settlement on Elizabeth Street. A proposal had been discussed about building a church structure on that site to make a permanent home for the Italian Mission Church. Funding for this project was not achieved. The cost of the lot was reported as $5,500. To the dismay of the Superintendent, it was noted that when funds were sought among the Epworth Leagues of the Methodist Churches, few responded. The Epworth League was a youth order of the Methodist Episcopal Church. Rev. Hammond lamented that *"the Epworth Leagues were more apt to pay money for the support or care of children in China or India than those locally"* (NNYC, 1910).

The work of the settlement met community needs and continued to grow. By 1910, twelve volunteers assisted Miss Davis with the program. They provided educational leadership in popular industrial and handwork classes. These classes often coincided with practical lessons in English and government; which helped the immigrant men to obtain citizenship.

Instrumental in the organization, and recognition of the need for settlement program by the NNYC, were the efforts of the *National Women's Home Missionary Society*. Gifts received for the thirtieth anniversary of the National Society increased the building fund (NNYC, 1924, Meeker, 1969). In 1910, work began on the building for the new location on Mary Street. The cornerstone was laid on November 3, 1910. Charlebois Brothers of Watertown, NY, had been awarded the contract. It was anticipated that the project would be completed in 1911.

Construction was delayed because of special foundation needs. Prior to the purchase of the land, the city of Utica had run conduit underneath the proposed site of the building. The conduit was to help divert an underground stream. The additional work that was needed for the foundation resulted in an extra expense of $800 (Smith, 2004). Today, the collapse of the conduit and the moisture from the underground water appear to be instrumental in the foundational collapse of the Mary Street building.

The Conference Report of 1911, prepared by Rev. J. B. Hammond, explained the importance of evangelizing to the foreigners located within the community. He reported that there were 35,000 Italians within the Conference who were accessible for Protestant evangelism. Hammond noted that an evening school to prepare the men for church membership was held four nights per week and a boys club two afternoons per week. The boys club had an average attendance of twenty-six (NNYC, 1911).

In May, 1912, Miss Davis and the other workers moved into the new Italian Settlement, at 615 Mary Street. Bishop William Burt dedicated the structure on Thursday, October 10, 1912 (Smith, 2004). In the annual report of 1912, Rev J. B. Hammond noted that *"although a great portion of the Italian adults are difficult to reach, their children are approachable, bright and lovable."* He reported that the property on Mary Street was free from all indebtedness (NNYC, 1912).

Under Miss Davis' leadership, and the dedicated support of her assistants, the programs grew and others were added. She established a Sunday School, the first Kindergarten program in Utica, sewing classes, and a boys club. Miss Davis also learned to speak some Italian, at least enough so that she could read the Bible to a group of mothers that gathered at the settlement house (Williams, 1980, Meeker, 1969).

The initial goals of the settlement were to teach immigrants to help themselves and sustain a lifestyle in which the family could function. The Queen Esther Circles, located in a number of Methodist churches in NNYC as part of the King's Daughters organization, continued to raise funds. A donation of $15 provided a full scholarship for the care of a child in the Settlement. This demonstrated the continued level of commitment that the Methodist women of the NNYC had for the success of the Settlement (Evans, 1998; Meeker, 1969).

Miss Davis (on left)

CHAPTER SEVEN
EARLY LEADERSHIP AND PROGRAMS

Following Miss Davis as superintendent to the Settlement was Miss Harriet Brown Taylor, succeeded by Miss Caroline P. Wilson. Historical data does not provide the length of their individual service.

Mrs. Alice Hunt of Adams, New York, is credited for a large part of the stability and growth of the settlement house. She served as the president of the NNYC Women's Home Missionary Society. Mrs. Hunt also served for nine years as president of the Italian Settlement's Board of Directors. When she retired from her board position, she noted in her formal farewell statement to the conference, in October, 1924, that the building was worth $50,000 and was debt-free (NNYC, 1924).

In personal correspondence to Settlement workers, Mrs. Hunt reflected on how the construction and opening of the Settlement had not been an easy task, especially since most of the efforts had been led by volunteers. She explained the challenges of financing all the operations, paying the contractors, and purchasing furniture while also paying salaries, and for the maintenance of the Settlement (Hunt, personal communication, 1929).

In 1924, because of the expanding program and the upkeep that was needed for the property, it was determined that a broader financial base was needed to support the Settlement. The Women's Home Missionary Society of the NNYC decided to transfer the property and the administration of the Settlement to their national Society. Under the direction of the national program, the Italian Settlement became one of the projects of the Methodist Church's Women's Division's Bureau for Foreign-Speaking People in the North (Meeker, 1969).

CHAPTER EIGHT
MISS HELEN MARIE EDICK

Miss Helen Marie Edick was appointed Director of the Settlement in 1927. Through her leadership, great strides in programming and public outreach were accomplished. Although still called the Italian Settlement, the community it served began to change. New immigrants flocked to the United States after World War I. The Italians were now joined by members of the Armenian, Syrian, Ukrainian, Polish and Jewish communities.

Miss Edick encouraged her workers to perform regular home visits, as she believed they were important in creating a bond of friendship between the Settlement and the families in the neighborhood. The programs and services offered by the Settlement kept pace with the changing needs of the community.

In the mid 1920's, when the Utica Public Schools established kindergarten programs within the school district, the Settlement House discontinued them. In 1928, the Settlement pioneered pre-school education by establishing the first nursery school program in the community. The program was a half-day session and was free for the children in the neighborhood. The nursery program was developed in response to the many undernourished three and four-year-olds that lived in the impoverished homes of the neighborhood. Because the Settlement provided a lunch with milk, as well as regular play and rest periods, the children began to improve physically and emotionally.

Girl Scout Troop No. 3 in the City of Utica was registered on March 21, 1929, with Helen Edick and Ruth Barnes listed as the Settlement House's troop leaders. Edick is listed as having joined the organization in 1927. It is not clear if this is the first troop at the Settlement or an additional troop. Most of the members listed lived in the 600 block of Mary Street and were in 4th – 6th grades.

As the United States struggled with the economic uncertainties of the Great Depression, the demand for services offered by settlement houses increased. Many immigrants became even more impoverished. As thousands of individuals across the country were unemployed, a greater number of women looked to the settlement house for employment. Personal correspondence to Helen Edick, from individuals seeking employment at the Settlement was available for this study. Among them is a letter from Rev. L. W. Hazen dated September 20, 1929, requesting that Miss Edick consider a placement for twenty-three year old Marian R. Miller, a four-year graduate of the State Teacher's College at Buffalo with a Bachelor of Science in Home Economics.

In 1929, Helen Edick began corresponding with Dorothy Norton. Norton wrote in a November 29th letter to Edick, that she had been referred by Miss Day, of Cincinnati, about the position as assistant kindergarten teacher at the Settlement. These examples of correspondence demonstrate the outreach and networking the settlement movement had on recruiting young women to service.

It is interesting to note that in December, 1929, a thank you letter from the *Elizabeth Marcy Center* in Chicago, Illinois, was sent to the Italian Settlement's *Queen Esther Girls*. The letter thanked them for the box of gifts that they sent to the children at the settlement in Chicago. The gifts were valued at $1.89. With the letter was a small photo brochure showing pictures of their Women's Home Missionary Society, some of the clubs offered to the children at that settlement, and photos of Chicago's ghetto. The Queen Esther Girls was one of the Italian Settlement House's circles. The connection to this agency in Chicago probably demonstrates an awareness of the Hull House in Chicago and Jane Addams. This act of charity by the children of the Italian Settlement was especially moving considering the economic conditions of their own neighborhood.

In June, 1930, a young college graduate, Philomena Brocardo (personal communication, June, n.d., 1930), wrote to Miss Edick stating, "After a very unsuccessful attempt to secure any form of employment, I am writing to ask if there is a position at the Settlement." Brocardo wrote about her B.S. degree in Home Economics, and her willingness to teach vocational classes in sewing and cooking. She also expressed an interest in music classes, having studied piano for five years. She acknowledged that she would expect only "sheets and pillow cases" for her room, assuming that a bed would be provided. For many women graduating college at that time, full-time paid positions were not always available. Many turned to volunteer service or to programs like the settlements where they would work for a small stipend, room and board (Barbuto, 1999).

Miss Edick looked throughout the NNYC for support and aid for the Settlement and relief for the children. In December, 1929, boxes from the Women's Auxiliary from the Methodist Church in Penn Yan, New York arrived. A letter from Mrs. A. C. Ansley, from the church to Miss Edick referenced the "two boxes, consisting of 33 quarts and 4 pints of fruit and vegetables, one jar of jelly and one peck of apples." Miss Ansley letter went on to state, " I can imagine seeing the children's eyes twinkle when they see the apples, which are scarce and of very poor quality this year. I will send you a list so you may know if any were removed from the boxes." (Ansley, personal communication, December, n.d., 1929).

A letter dated July 12, 1930, from Caroline M. Ames, who was part of the Executive Committee for Camp Dempster, a Methodist summer facility, reflected a request that Miss Edick make plans to attend a meeting to discuss children from the Settlement attending camp the following summer. The proposed meeting was a result of the success of the previous summer's camp, and the correspondence reflected on how much the young girls at the Settlement seemed to enjoy the experience.

In the 1929-1930 Settlement House's Annual Report prepared by Miss Edick, she reported that the paid staff had grown to six, and that the Settlement currently served 175 families living within three blocks of the Settlement. She stated that,

> *...three blocks away, and parallel to us are several hundred families that have had no Settlement or Christian influence. In past year, our interest has been in those immediately surrounding us because we are thickly populated. But the past ten years have greatly benefited the living conditions and morale of our people and the time is now ripe for us to push out a little farther and aid those within our vicinity who have hitherto been untouched* (Edick, 1930).

In the Settlement's 1932-1933 Annual Report, Miss Edick detailed what might have been seen in one of the vocational cooking classes,

> *...you could have caught a glimpse of Palma as she entered the Cooking department last fall. She came, not because she was financially able to pay the very small fee, but because her faithfulness in Sunday School had earned her the privilege. She stood there, shabby, undernourished, underweight and altogether*

quite hopeless in appearance. There are many children in Palma's family and the mother tries very hard to make the altogether too small amount go around. Her father is almost blind and work is not easy to secure. We will never forget the eagerness, delight and gratitude in Palma's eyes as she stood there. To her, cooking meant a chance to learn something and a chance to have something good to eat... (Edick, 1933).

In the early 1930's, Italian women who had benefited from the services of the Italian Settlement House, and had achieved success through education and business endeavors, formed the Nita Kola Service Club. In 1936, the Club's service project was to financially support the new nursery program offered at the Settlement. The nursery school is still in operation today.

Available to young women at the Settlement were the Opportunity and Fidelity Circles, chapters of the King's Daughters organization. In a notebook dated 1935, minutes from one of the meetings (n.d.) indicate that Miss Edick was thanked by the members for giving direction and program suggestions.

The Settlement House focused on many vocational education projects. Under Miss Edick's guidance, a strong Home Economics program had been established. Many of the young women of the neighborhood married in their mid-teens, often dropping out of high school to begin their domestic lives. The Settlement offered classes in meal preparation, sewing, budgeting, and household management. Working mothers and girls employed in the local factories would meet during the week for an evening of fellowship and practical application to the skills taught in the classes.

The mothers that stayed at home to tend to the needs of the family would meet twice a week to repair or modify clothing and accessories for their families. Some would make-over clothes found during a rummage sale or cut up potato sacks and use the material to sew underwear. Women learned the art of loom weaving and made rugs for the cold floors of their tenement apartments. The classes would end with devotions, and hymn singing was encouraged as the women worked (Evans, 1998; Meeker, 1969).

Along with the programs for the neighborhood women, there were clubs and classes for all ages of boys, plus activities for men.

Volunteers from the local YMCA would help the staff at the settlement. As wholesome recreation gained in popularity, fewer instances of petit larceny and general mischief by the boys in the neighborhood were reported. Programs including scouting and a basketball team used the recreation room. Outings to local swimming pools were held in the summer, as well as hiking and bicycle trips along the Utica Parkway.

Men took carpentry classes and learned to make double and triple-decker beds. This was a necessity when large families, often with six or more children, would have to crowd into small two or three-room flats. A critical item made in the wood working classes was the crisis box. It was used like a modern day safe or bank security box. Families would store in the crisis box important documents such as baptism and citizenship papers, marriage licenses, treasured family pictures or other heirlooms.

Children's Music Lessons

CHAPTER NINE
MISS RUTH WRIGHT

Miss Ruth Wright joined the staff in 1929. Her annual salary was $600. Miss Edict, the Director, received $673 per year. Miss Wright was a strong supporter of the arts and hoped to provide an opportunity for each individual to express and develop their natural artistic talent. She believed that art added new dimensions to the lives of the people that the Settlement served. The art classes that Miss Wright taught included practical skills. She led groups in block printing, dyeing, woodworking, weaving, and jewelry making. Some of the class members sold items they had created to help bring financial relief to their families. Wright's training and background were varied. She had trained as an occupational therapist. During her tenure with the Settlement, her accomplishments included social work, developing skills as a draftsman, learning carpentry skills, and she studied business administration.

During the fall of each year, an Interest Finder was given to the community members. This survey listed all the proposed activities and described the different types of clubs and classes that could be offered at the Settlement. Neighborhood members were asked to check the items that would most interest them. From this survey, the Settlement program was developed to meet the needs and interests of the people it served. Certain classes appeared to be favorites, and were regularly included in the Settlement's schedule. Among those classes were the Marionette Club, Dramatics, Handicraft Specialties, and the Glee Club (Meeker, 1969).

Each Christmas, the Settlement was alive with activity. Children and adults joined together for weeks of carol singing, Christmas plays, hanging of the greens, and decorating cookies for the children. The women's groups at many of the Methodist churches in the NNYC donated items, including hand-knitted mittens, to distribute to the children.

Family conflicts often arose as the gap widened between "old world" parents and their American-born children. Counseling, therefore, was an on-going mission. Generations struggled to merge the customs and values of the parents with the new standards and ethics of the children who were trying to make their way and fit in with the youth in the community. Parents constantly worried that their sons would become involved with criminal behavior and that their daughters were trying to express their independence. Americanization classes helped to develop a better understanding. The Italian Settlement was truly a melting pot where different nationalities, races, ages, and customs could meet in fellowship (Evans, 1998; Meeker, 1969).

Miss Helen Marie Edick – first row – center
Miss Ruth Wright – second row, second from left

CHAPTER TEN
THE NEIGHBORHOOD CENTER

In 1945, Ruth Wright was named the Settlement's Executive Director. She initiated changing the name of the *Italian Settlement House* to *The Neighborhood Center* (Williams, 1980). Miss Wright believed that this new name better suited the ethnic diversity that the area had experienced over the past few decades. Ruth Wright was one of the first social workers in the city to be elected to the Academy of Certified Social Workers and was a charter member of the National Association of Social Workers.

Ruth recognized the need for a safe and well-maintained playground for the Center. Children, darting in and out of narrow spaces between buildings, and into the street, were a safety concern. Without organized play, the children were often seen marking buildings and dumping trash containers. They also scaled fences and irritated neighbors by ringing doorbells and running away. Wright believed that these actions, on the part of the children, were a natural reaction to being confined in small, crowded dwellings that often housed six to twenty families.

Adjacent to the Neighborhood Center was an empty lot that was owned by the NNYC. In 1947, Miss Wright challenged the people of the neighborhood to meet the needs of the children and to build a playground for them. A three-day festival was organized to raise funds. Groups created crafts and other items to sell at the festival. The effort were supported by the local press who rallied for the impoverished neighborhood that chose to work for an improvement, rather than asking for it to be given to them. Publicity from this project heightened the awareness of the services of the Center throughout the community. The festival was very successful both financially and in terms of fellowship (Wright, 1948).

Miss Wright believed that an individual's positive self-esteem was essential in being prepared to meet the more pressing challenges of life with limited incomes. An article printed in the Utica Observer-Dispatch (OD) in 1952, highlights a hat-making class led by Miss Wright. It reported that twenty-five women enrolled in the class, ranging in age from teenagers to grandmothers. All were quite proud of the fashion accessory that they had created and the money they were able to save their families ("One Way To Beat High Prices of Hats", 1952). This was one example of using vocational education to enhance the skills of the participants.

The Neighborhood Center expanded its relationships with the New York State Department of Education (NYDOE) and with colleges that offered majors in education. In 1952, six hundred seventy adults received vocational training at the Center. Classes included ceramics, metal crafts, and clothing construction. The instructors were hired with funds provided by the NYDOE's Adult Education Division. Working within the paradigm of education, students from the State Institute of Agriculture and Home Economics at Cobleskill, New York, came to the Settlement for cooperative fieldwork. One intern was Marion Schafer, a senior majoring in Early Childhood Development at Cobleskill, who came to work in the Nita Kola Nursery ("She'll Study at Center", 1952).

In an effort to continue the Settlement's tradition of health care education to the community, the Center invited prominent local medical professionals, such as Dr. James Rose, to speak at regular monthly meetings held for the parents of the nursery children. These activities were forerunners of educational policies established by programs like Head Start in the 1960's. The Center was the first agency in Utica to initiate a Head Start program.

The creation and use of marionettes had been a favorite activity for the teens at the Center. Miss Wright made many efforts to help the youth of the Center realize that they were part of a much larger community. She established contact with Señor Ernesto Cadiquada, Director of the Pestalozzi City Schools, in Florence, Italy. The city of Florence was still healing from the effects of WWII. Due to limited post-war supplies, children's toys in Italy were considered a luxury. Five boxes of food, clothing, and toys, including hand-made puppets, were collected as part of the *Hanging of the Greens* program at the Center during December, 1951. These items were shipped to the school in Florence. Senor Cadiquada wrote back to express their appreciation and the delight of the children with the toys, clothing, food, and particularly with the puppets, which had been made by the King's Daughters group of the Center ("Puppets Hailed by Italian Tots," 1952).

An article in the Utica newspaper included information about the leadership skills of a 16 year-old who participated in the Center's 4-H program. The youth had been newly elected, Editor-in-Chief of the New

York State 4-H Club Council newspaper. She was also recognized as a leader among her peers by offering help with the younger girls at the Center in the cooking, sewing, and home improvement classes (Price, 1952).

Miss Wright organized a fund-raising drive with the Center's House Council and raised sixty-one dollars to buy and ship a goat to a family in Korea ("They Get Our Goat," 1952). Wright also initiated health education in tuberculosis as well as a bicycle safety program.

Young girls selling cookies in support of a Settlement fund raiser

CHAPTER ELEVEN
MISS MARIE RUSSO

On March 9, 1955, the Neighborhood Center issued a news release announcing the appointment of Marie Russo as the group work program director. Her appointment would begin in September of that year. Russo, who was completing graduate work at Columbia University, had worked as the summer playground director for four years and as a group worker at the Center since 1952, during her college breaks.

In 1957, Miss Russo developed the *Junior Citizens for Community Improvement Club* at the Center. The neighborhood had been experiencing an exodus of the tightly knit Italian community that had resided there for multiple generations. More and more transient families were coming in, and homes that had been privately owned were now becoming rental properties. The teen-based Junior Citizen's Program would patrol the neighborhood and voluntarily clean lots and home fronts in an attempt to improve the condition of their neighborhood. As they completed the work, they would leave a flyer at the home encouraging the resident to keep the area clean and neat (Neighborhood Center, 1957).

Houses had been bought at bargain prices and many were owned by absentee landlords. In response to the changing demographics, and the lack of commitment on the part of the landlords, Miss Wright led her staff in social action for housing codes enforcement. The action angered a number of local politicians and could have adversely affected local funding for the agency.

Ruth Wright's last full year of service came in 1966. The neighborhood had experienced many changes since her arrival in 1929. In her report for the Center's May annual meeting, Miss Wright noted that the Center's Head Start program would double in size over the next program year. Staff were conducting workshops and in-service training programs for Head Start teachers, aides, and Youth Corps personnel. Staff members participated in the Pre-School Enrichment Committee and the Utica Community Action Commission. The Neighborhood Center had provided on-the-job experience and training for students in the Work Study Programs from two local colleges. Literacy classes and other educational opportunities were planned. The annual operating budget of the agency was $51,599.67. The staff included 6 full-time personnel, and

32 part-time personnel. The playground had been used 7,434 times by neighborhood children during that summer and 1,442 different individuals had received services during the year (Neighborhood Center, 1966).

Marie Russo was named Executive Director in 1967. She implemented additional programs. Her first year saw the beginning of the summer day camp programs.

In 1969, Anne Westwood from London, who was attending Chiswick Polytechnic College, chose to complete a summer internship at the Neighborhood Center. Westwood was involved with the settlement programs in England, and lived at the Bishop Creighton House in London. She wanted to compare the settlement life in London with America's. According to an interview that she gave for the United Methodist publication, *Response*, this was a positive experience for her (Response, 1969). Anne Westwood was not the only international personality at the Center. She and full-time staff worker, Esther Ang, from Hong Kong, worked together on an enrichment program for 9 – 11 year-olds. The activity, *Know Your City*, introduced the children to places like the City Hall, the local newspaper, an industrial plant, the telephone company, and museums. Westwood expressed the humor in two foreign women leading the city awareness expedition (Response, 1969).

Under the leadership of Marie Russo, programs continued to be developed. The *Career Development Trainee Program* began in 1969. A thrift store opened in 1974 in an additional property purchased by the Center. In 1975, a casework department was opened and a school-based program, *Partners in Prevention*, was begun in 1977. The program was designed to aid in dropout prevention. Two agency vans were purchased, one in 1975 and the other in 1977. A *Youth Employment Network* was started in 1978. Students from the State University of New York conducted an economic research study of the families that used the services of the Neighborhood Center in 1976. The study reported that the mean income was $6,930 - $7,649 with 16.8% of the families below poverty level (Bakey, 1976).

Highlighting the seventy-fifth anniversary of the agency in 1980, was the consecration of their new youth center, built at a cost of $942,000. The building housed a day care center, group work facilities, adult activity areas, a thrift shop, and a recreational room. Bishop Joseph Yeakel, of the United Methodist Church, presided at the consecration service. He noted the uniqueness of the Center among other Methodist agencies in the NNYC, and the longevity of the program. Utica Mayor, Stephen Pawlinga, issued a proclamation declaring the day as *Neighborhood Center Day* (Maurizio, 1980). The building was dedicated to the memory of former Executive Director, Ruth Wright, who had passed away in 1977. Miss Wright had given forty-two years of service to the Center. At the dedication ceremonies, Neighborhood Center Board Chairman, Clifford Frey, made a special tribute to Miss Marie Russo, as he discussed Russo's vision of the services that would be provided in the new building (Williams, 1980).

As part of the Center's 1980 Annual Report, Chairman Frey noted that the effectiveness of the programs at the Neighborhood Center have resulted in a participant increase from 1000 members per year in the 1950's to over 5000 members in 1979 (Frey, 1980). While many of the programs and services had remained consistent over the years, the 1980's brought an additional element to the services offered by the Neighborhood Center. Departments were added in social group work, casework, youth employment, and a community support system for mental patients who had been assimilated back into the community from the Utica Psychiatric Center (Williams, 1980). The 2000 Annual Report noted that in 1999 - 2000, the Neighborhood Center served a large metropolitan and rural area and its programs touched the lives of more than 26,326 people (Neighborhood Center, 2000).

Miss Marie A. Russo

CHAPTER TWELVE
MOVING FORWARD

Beginning as the Italian Settlement House, the Center has provided over one hundred years of service to the Utica community. The agency provides a wide variety of activities and programming. Currently included in their services, is an after-school enrichment program for school-aged youth ages 5-17. This program incorporates such components as personal growth, character building, violence and drug prevention, creative arts, career and technical education, computer literacy, team building, and social development. The educational component provides academic assistance and school outreach services to help high risk students achieve success in school (Neighborhood Center, Inc., 2009).

Social workers and counselors in the Center's Behavioral Healthcare Services provide assistance in child guidance. The Center's professionals work with clinics, schools, and in homes to provide services to families, children, and adolescents. The agency's *School Partnership for Youth* program provides school-based preventative services to children and families. *The Mobile Crisis Assessment Team* (MCAT) provides crisis services for children and adults in New York's Oneida and Herkimer counties on weekends and holidays.

For young, school-aged children, the Neighborhood Center provides day camps during winter, spring, and summer breaks from school. The youth component provides local pre-teens and teens an opportunity for growth in character development and life skills. Appropriate developmental activities are designed to advance and promote positive social behaviors and life-style choices (Neighborhood Center, Inc., 2009).

Marie Russo as a teen, with the after school children's group she led

Marie (center) with Glee Club helping to select new music

CHAPTER THIRTEEN
AN ORAL HISTORY – MARIE RUSSO

The dedication plaque on the entrance door of the Neighborhood Center's Marie A. Russo Conference Center, their main headquarters which is now located on Genesee Street in Utica reads: *"In recognition of a woman whose vision, generosity, commitment and love have made the world a better place."*

It is no wonder then, that Marie's legacy holds many honors and awards including:

- Social Worker of Year
- Business and Professional Woman of the Year
- Outstanding Citizen Award from the League of Women Voters
- The Harmony and Cultural Integrity Award from the Utica Chapter of the International Mediation Society
- The Martin Luther King, Jr. Award for Citizenship
- Community Service Award from the New York State Division for Youth
- The Lifetime Achievement Award from the National Association of Social Workers.

Nor is it a surprise that she has earned diplomas from Morningside College and Columbia University, or that she has served on the Utica Public School's Board of Education. What would surprise most are the obstacles that she overcame that led to her many accomplishments.

Through the oral histories that follow, Marie provides her personal insights into her relationship with the early years of the Italian Settlement, and her reflections on the significance of the agency in her life.

CHAPTER FOURTEEN
NARRATIVE ONE: MARIE RUSSO'S PERCEPTION OF HER EARLY LIFE IN UTICA, NEW YORK

I grew up in Utica, New York. East Utica was the section of the city where most of the Italian refugees settled. The neighborhood had low-income housing; the buildings were cheap for the landlords to keep, but the rent took up more than half of my parents' income. Most of the parents in my neighborhood worked in the mills, on the railroad, or doing low wage labor-type jobs. Italians were the biggest group of immigrants to Utica. Over 15,000 of the men that worked on the Erie Canal were Italian immigrants or their children. There were also Arabic speaking groups like the Syrian, Lebanese, and Armenians. Utica was a big melting pot. The next wave of immigrants brought the Germans, Ukrainians, and the Polish.

When immigrants first came to the Utica area, they settled in areas that reflected their own ethnic pocket. They formed little colonies; that is why the Settlement was first called the Italian Colony Settlement.

Utica, and the small towns around it, had come to life with the Industrial Revolution. Companies like Harden Furniture, Savage Arms, the Utica Knitting Company, the railroad and the canal had all drawn immigrants to the area. While the bosses and owners of the mills made fortunes, it was not reflected in the wages and the treatment of the immigrant and hourly workers. This, and economic factors like the Depression, the wars, all resulted in causing a lot of the poverty in my neighborhood.

I lived on Third Avenue, in a building that had been designed to be a four family apartment house. The landlord had added more walls to some of the units to make more apartments. There were about twenty different families living in the building. They weren't all families; some were drunks, prostitutes, and men with dark, piercing eyes that watched you climb the steps to your doorway; men who lurked in the shadows and had evil in their hearts. I used to have to yell up to my mother from the street, "Ma, meet me at the door," because I was afraid to go into my building alone. It was very traumatic.

Our apartment was small and there wasn't any room to store things. We could put some things in the cellar, but it was dirty and damp and there was no protection from theft. I was not supposed to go down there alone, because sometimes homeless people would squat there. The house also had a sub-basement. A lot of bootleg booze was hidden in the sub-basement during and after Prohibition. Some of the houses in the neighborhood had underground tunnels where bootleggers could roll barrels of homemade liquor and wine underground towards the Canal. Rats, some of them the size of cats, lived in the sub-basement.

Our building was infested with cockroaches, bed bugs and everyone had head lice. If you see photos of women and girls with big handkerchiefs tied around their heads, it was to keep them from either catching lice, or to keep others from catching it from them. There were a lot of kids. Most families were big, like mine. If you went two blocks in every direction from the Settlement, there would probably have been over one hundred fifty kids.

The buildings were very close to each other. In some, you could reach out of the window and scrape your nails along the outside wall next door. Some of the buildings had small backyards. This land was treated like gold because people could plant small gardens and grow food. For the houses with gardens, there would be just little pathways to get between them. There was no room for kids to play in yards, so we had to play in the street.

Multifamily dwelling on Mary Street

CHAPTER FIFTEEN
NARRATIVE TWO: MARIE RUSSO'S PERCEPTION OF HER EARLY EXPERIENCES AT THE SETTLEMENT

My mother did not go to the Center except for things that affected the children; you know rummage sales, things like that. She did not do anything much with the adult groups of women. She did not have time with all the little ones at home and our father liked her to be home, not out with other people.

I came to the Center when I was six. My best friend, Katie, the Valenti girls, and a whole bunch of kids from the street was already going over to the Settlement House. I wanted a closer look.

Diagonally from my house, I could see the settlement on Mary Street. My mother had never said we could not go, but I knew better than to ask. It was easier to beg for forgiveness than it was for permission. If she had said no, and I went anyway, then I would be beat for disobedience, and my parents would dig in and I would never be allowed to go. I was still at the age when I listened to what my mother said.

I remember Katie telling me one afternoon that she was going over to the Settlement, so I went with her. Miss Foster, a great big woman, met us at the door and invited us to come upstairs to join the others for a little recreation. I didn't trust her, I didn't trust anybody, but I went inside. I will never forget that Miss Foster, a big, strapping woman, got down on her knees. She held her arms out in a very welcoming way. The welcomes I usually got from people were the kinds of gestures where the finger points and angry voices tell you to get the heck away from their property. So, to have this tall, large woman literally get on her knees so she could look into our faces was incredible. And we were not intimidated by her height because she was looking us in the eyes, and smiling, and nodding her head.

The thing I remember most about the first time that I went to the Settlement House was the unusual experience of feeling loved, unconditionally. I can't really explain it. The Settlement was like a place where you could go and feel valued, loved and no one ridiculed you for having "foreign ways." And I was not exactly the kind of kid that was easy to love. I didn't trust anybody and I certainly did not believe them when they said they cared about who and what I was.

We followed Miss Foster up to this room. We had to walk up steps to get to where we went in, about 20 steps or so. They were very clean. You could tell that someone swept them every day. We went through these wooden doors into a hall and then into a room. She left us for a few minutes, and when she came back she brought out a big plate of cookies; oatmeal cookies, and chocolate milk.

I just grabbed them by the handful and stuffed them into my mouth. One of the things I remember so well was that she was never judgmental or critical about our style. She said to us, "*you know we are never going to run out of cookies - we have so many of them in the kitchen and all the milk you can drink - it would be okay to take one cookie at a time and we will keep filling up the plate any time it is empty.*" After that, Katie and I went on a regular basis to the Center.

When I was six, my sister, Liz (Elizabeth), was one, my brother, Carmen, was three, Eleanor was seven and my brother, Sammy, was nine. My sister, Linda, was born many years later - she was the surprise in the family. After we began going to the Settlement, my sister, Eleanor, attended some of the sewing classes there. She also went to the cooking classes and brought some of those skills back home. She would make tapioca pudding, scalloped potatoes, or a white cake she learned to cook there, and she would help with the family sewing. Our mother had real health issues, so Eleanor really took care of us. She learned the skills she needed to do that at the Settlement.

We called the women that worked there, "teachers" and, at first, it made it difficult for me to trust and turn to them. Thankfully, they did not turn from me. More and more, I began to go over to the Settlement House.

I got involved with a lot of the after-school programs. They had youth clubs and activities for us. We would square dance. I was in the Red Bird Club, the Blue Bird Club, Mother's Jewels, Home Guards, sewing, woodworking, chorus, and they taught us puppetry in the Marionette Club. The teachers there even arranged for us to go on trips, like to New York City. The Italian Settlement House became a haven that I became more and more familiar with. The first hot shower I ever had in my life, was at the Settlement.

In the summer, we could go to Camp Dempster for fifty cents a week. The camp was owned by the Methodist Church and was somewhere on Oneida Lake. The deaconess at the Settlement rented camp space there. The teachers at camp were volunteers from the "Queen Esther" chapter of the King's Daughters. We would be brought there by truckloads. Kids from our neighborhood did not even know we were that close to a lake. For the first time, we would learn how to swim. At night, we would have campfires and sing camp songs. We went on nature trails. We would bond and dare to begin to dream dreams. It was a refuge from the poverty and sorrow we all lived in. It helped to make us more sensitive to the world around us.

Through the Settlement, we began to understand for the first time what real compassion and caring was. It was the teachers who helped inspire, cultivate, and liberate us. The Settlement helped me to get in touch with the power, the hope, and the potential that was within me.

When Miss Edick was the director, she organized a hymn singing program on Sunday afternoons. I liked to sing, and she did some little Bible stories too. It was very informal. We would gather and have some hot chocolate and cookies, and then Miss Edick or someone would begin to play the piano. The settlement had a Sunday School and a Sunday Hour of Gospel, but we did not usually go to those, just the afternoon gathering. I liked it because the stories were in English, not Latin like our church, so you could understand it.

The Settlement became our refuge. It was a haven. They even hired me to be a janitor and to clean it. I was probably ten or twelve years old. They would give me just some little jobs to do so I would have a couple of bucks a week. I think they did it just because they knew how things were at home, but they never said anything. Food was scarce at home, and sometimes I would sneak into the Center's kitchen and steal fruit. There were always cookies in the cookie jar and there was always milk, and they knew I was taking it. How can you not be in love with a place like that? It just made it possible to survive. I used to get Irene, my cousin, to do the dusting and some of the other cleaning. Because I was making $2.80 a week, I paid her a dollar to do the work and I kept the $1.80 [laughs].

I had tremendous people helping me when I was a kid at the Settlement. Every year, Christmas was a special celebration. There would be a "Hanging of the Greens" program, and we would have special treats, snacks and eggnog. We would sing songs, and there was usually a little Christmas play. There would be a package under the tree at the Center for me. We didn't have those things at home; for a long time there were no new things for us, no presents. Our parents did not have the means.

The King's Daughters groups from the different Methodist churches would make mittens to hang on the Christmas tree as special gifts for the neighborhood children. At one of the programs, I got my first pair of mittens, hat, scarf, and warm things to wear that I never had before. I got my first doll and my first patent leather shoes that nobody else had ever worn but me.

One Christmas break, when I was a little older, Miss Dorothy Norton, who was in charge of the nursery school program, took me to her home in Olean, NY, to make a special Christmas for me. Miss Norton had been a teacher with the Buffalo School District and had attended the Hartford Seminary Foundation before she came to the settlement.

Marie in the Settlement's choir (second row center – with glasses)

Marie (broom) and other youth cleaning Mary Street

CHAPTER SIXTEEN
NARRATIVE THREE: MARIE RUSSO'S PERCEPTION OF PUBLIC EDUCATION DURING HER YOUTH

The Settlement was where we really learned the skills that we needed to survive: skills like cooking and sewing, eating right, bathing, and tutors to help get us through math and English, because our parents were unable to help us with homework.

Our public schools were overcrowded, and only two of Utica's primary schools and the high school had a gymnasium. My school did not have one, but the Settlement had a small gymnasium in the basement. It provided recreational basketball and other team activities for the children. The playgrounds at the schools were small and very limited with equipment.

School was very painful and humiliating. The teachers of the public schools were judgmental and condemning towards the children of the refugees. None of us had decent clothing, and we did not bathe regularly. The teachers would walk up and down our classroom rows. I knew what they were looking for. Glancing at our heads, they would stop at some of our desks. They always stopped at mine. The teacher would take her ruler and lift my hair, inspecting me for head lice. I seemed to never fail her test. After a while, she started lifting my hair with a yardstick. She so obviously did not want to get any nearer to me then she had too.

There was nothing you could do about the head lice. My mother worked very hard at night to get the lice out of our hair. But with cold water flats and hallway toilets, no matter what she did, you could not get rid of your lice. Even if you did, in a couple of days you would have them again. My mother would soak our hair with kerosene and vinegar, and then tie a large rag around our head. The smell lasted forever. The kids in public schools would not play with us, and the smell and bandanas only increased their ridicule. We also had to wear little sacks of garlic around our necks. Our mother thought it would chase away evil spirits, but all they did was add to the cruelty from the kids in our school.

I was pretty much a school dropout. I was, and would have stayed one, except for the wonderful women at the Settlement House. Ruth Wright, from Vermont, and Melva Tiemens, from Iowa, were my mentors and inspiration. When they learned that I was going to quit school, they interceded. They talked with my parents and convinced them of my potential. There used to be a conflict between many of the immigrant parents on the need for the children to go to high school. Many students dropped out of school between the 6th and 8th grade. Quitting school and getting a job to help support the family was more important. That is why Ruth and

Melva had to go and speak to my parents, to convince them that I should be allowed to stay in school

Melva worked at the Settlement for two years. During that time, this wonderful teacher, friend to all of us kids, encouraged me and made that connection with me that for the first time let me have some capacity to dream and feel as if there was some direction to my life. She saw something in me that was beyond whatever I knew myself could ever be. Because of this wonderful teacher, I began to find that where I once had rage and anger, I was beginning to feel peace and a sense of purpose.

Melva Tiemens organized one of the greatest adventures I ever had. She planned a summer bike trip that would take us through the New England states. We covered over 600 miles and stayed at youth hostels. I had never realized how vast the world was and how beautiful nature could be. Nine of us participated. The boys checked the bikes and made sure they were in working order. The girls would shop for supplies and make meals. It was hard work, but the memories of that trip will live with me forever.

Melva had graduated from Morningside College in Sioux City, Iowa, and inspired in me the dream that I, too, could go to college. Ruth also wanted me to go, and believed I could be successful. But that meant I would have to go and finish high school. I did not want to let them down, so, at the age of 17, I entered the ninth grade. I had to get through Algebra, Latin and Spanish. It was not easy.

There were some incredible people rooting for me, praying for me. Mrs. Schermerhorn and Mrs. Hollenbeck were two of my teachers and they went to Central Methodist Church. They tried to help me; they gave me the tools I needed to earn good marks and tried to talk to the other teachers at Proctor High School.
I graduated high school with a 94 average, in the top 10 of my class, and a member of the National Honor Society. With Melva's strong recommendation, Morningside College accepted my application. With the support of my family and the Methodist Church, I was able to attend Morningside. Poppa agreed to help me financially for my first year. When I got cold feet about leaving Utica and going to Iowa, Poppa packed my bags, drove me to the railroad station, and made sure I got on the train. I thank him every day of my life for doing that.

In 1952, I completed a Bachelor of Arts degree and graduated college magna cum laude. I was elected to Alpha Kappa Delta, the national honorary sociological society. I served as vice-president of Pi Gamma Mu, national honorary social sciences fraternity and Zeta Sigma, Morningside's honorary scholastic fraternity.

After graduation, I did an internship at the Neighborhood Center. Because of the internship, I was awarded a full scholarship to Columbia University. The scholarship was given to someone who could demonstrate that they had the talent, will, *and dedication required for the field of Social Work. My year of volunteering at the Center showed that. I earned my Master's degree from Columbia University in 1955.*

Years later, I was a guest preacher at Poland Methodist Church. I was sharing the story about getting a test back, and as the paper was being handed to me I saw a zero, but when the hand moved there was a nine in front of the zero and I passed. In the congregation, a head moved and I realized that the teacher was sitting in the pew. She smiled at me, and after the service we hugged, and then we both cried.

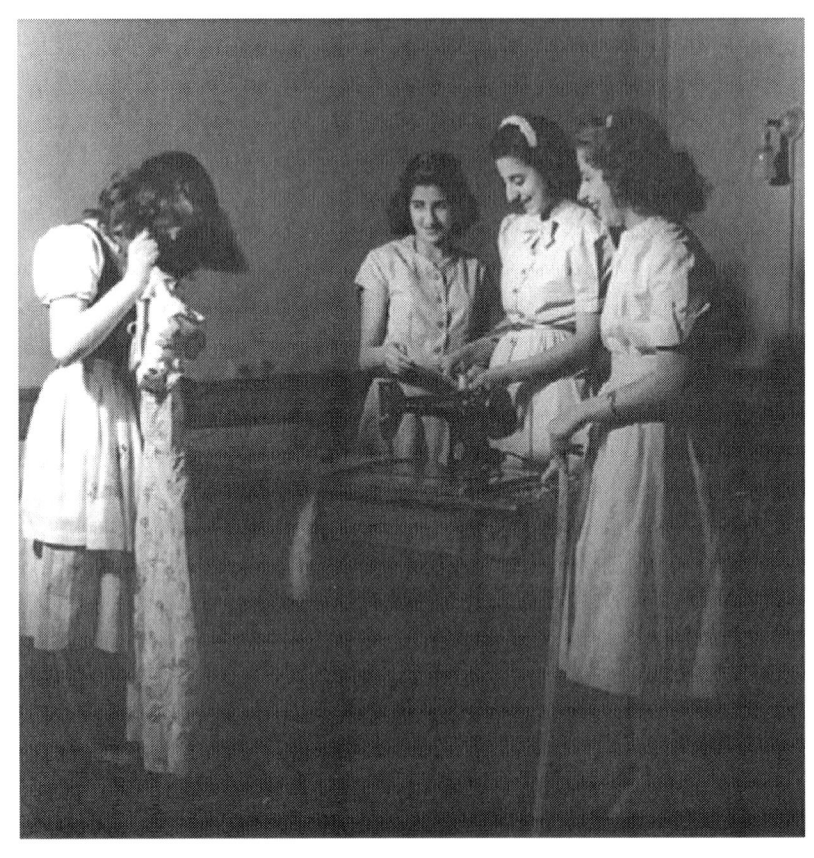

Young ladies participating in sewing class

CHAPTER SEVENTEEN
NARRATIVE FOUR: MARIE RUSSO'S PERCEPTION OF THE EARLY HISTORY OF THE SETTLEMENT

I can't tell you everything about the early years, just the stuff off the top of my head. All the records are at the Center. Mary Hightower and I tried to piece together a history; it is about ten pages long and we tried to list important dates and events from the past.

Back then, and even when I was the director, we were always so short handed, taking the time to record everything was just not possible. I wish now we had. I don't think anyone has ever really researched who we were and what we did, and it is all so important. Everything was just passed down kind of word of mouth. Maybe because I was always there, the staff just thought I knew; we just did not talk about it.

We began in 1905. New York had a lot of industry, factories, and there were thousands of immigrants, many Italian, who came to America and worked in our factories. A lot of them came to Utica, and did not speak any English, and they wanted to be American citizens. A group of church women got together and set up offices to teach English to the immigrants and help them file for citizenship papers. These women recognized an even bigger need and approached their church for additional support.

I believe that there have been five directors; I was the fourth one. I can tell you all I know about Ruth Wright. She was wonderful, and I loved her dearly. She was my mentor and my friend. I can tell what I can about the first two, but it is a bit sketchy, and there are limited records available. There are some boxes in the attic of the Mary Street building.

Miss Edick was the first director that I knew, but there was a lady before her, I did not know her personally and I am not sure of her name, I heard the name "Alice Hunt" often. It might have been her. If it wasn't, then I know that Miss Hunt was important to the early days. Miss Edick was a deaconess of the Methodist Church, and when she left the center she became a Professor of Theology at Hartford Seminary. Many of the women who were so instrumental to the history of the Settlement were Methodist Deaconesses of the Home Missionary Society. The Methodist church owned the building and was really in charge of the mission. They still own most of the property, so it was mainly staffed, especially back then, by Methodist people. And most of the funding came from the Methodist Church.

The staff of the Center was all women. For many women back then, even if they had a college degree, it was not socially acceptable for them to work. A lot of them did things through their church and in the social work field. The church was the only acceptable way that society would let them spread their wings and do the things they were capable of. I want you to be sure to write about what the churches did, especially the Women's Division of the Methodist Church, to get our Center going. Occasionally a man would work part time with the boys groups, especially the basketball team. Sometimes the Center would partner up with a program or a man from the YMCA or the Boys Club.

The staff of the Center offered help in the naturalization process. In the early years, the settlement also had lessons in English. Then classes began in homemaking, cooking, and sewing for the immigrant women. The Center also had a medical dispensary and had the first kindergarten class in Utica. Because so many of the immigrants had to live in dirty, filthy tenements, the Center even had a place where they could come and bathe. Lots of them had to share one bathroom where they lived. There might be seven or eight families all trying to use the same bathroom and not too much hot water, if any.

Children on the "new" playground

CHAPTER EIGHTEEN
NARRATIVE FIVE: MARIE RUSSO'S PERCEPTIONS OF KEY SETTLEMENT STAFF THAT SHE FEELS WERE INFLUENTIAL IN HER LIFE

Miss Edick was the Director when I was a child. She was a Deaconess in the Methodist Church. In addition to the programs offered by the Settlement, she organized religious services, including Sunday School and hymn sings. She openly expressed her religious beliefs and theology. Bad language was a particular issue with her; children who repeatedly swore or used the Lord's name in vain would promptly have their mouths washed out with soap. Miss Edick left the settlement to become a Professor at Hartford College.

Miss Ruth Wright succeeded Miss Edick. She had arrived in 1929. In 1945, she was named the Executive Director. I always admired Miss Edick, but it was Miss Wright that I loved. I still do. She was my mentor, my guardian, and my friend. She inspired me in so many ways and taught me to look beyond the city blocks that made up my world. She taught me that responsibility was a global calling. Ruth made me realize the potential that was within me.

Ruth was one of nine children and her father was a dairyman. She graduated from Albany Business College and for four years taught business and secretarial science classes at the Folts Institute in Herkimer, NY. After that, she went back to college and earned a degree in Occupational Therapy from the University of Philadelphia. She completed graduate training in the New York School of Social Work and took courses at different schools to enhance whatever interest or skills she wanted to focus on.

Ruth took classes at Oxbow, Vermont; New York University at Chautauqua; and the William Dickson School of Design, which is located in New York City. She also studied at Plymouth Meeting in Pennsylvania, and the Augustus F. Rose Rhode Island School of Design. She always felt that learning should be a life-long goal, and that students should explore all topics and areas to expand their mind and their soul.

Ruth did amazing things and she did things that a lot of people thought were "men's work". Remember, this was long before the 1970's and Title IX and equal rights. During the Second World War, she served as a design draftsman and instructor at Rome Air Force Base. She did all this while working at the Settlement. The Settlement House was open all year, but the clubs and programs met for blocks of time. Since many of the teachers were volunteers, or worked for barely anything, the time blocks allowed them time to pursue other interests. Some needed to have a supplemental job to help meet their financial needs. Ruth was a life-long learner who continued her professional development in whatever area that could aid others.

I remember that Ruth was an avid reader, and would turn to books and magazines to help her learn about new trends in child development, or to find craft ideas that she could teach in class. The Instructor, Popular Homecraft, Popular Mechanics and Pilgrim Elementary Teacher were among her favorites.

Ruth loved her summer home in Pawlet, Vermont. It was a big, beautiful, Victorian home with a lot of early American antiques. The home had been left to her by her aunt. Ruth and her family often spent time together there. Ruth was so engaged with us at the Center, her duties as Director, and with her many other pursuits, it made her infrequent trips to Vermont and time with her family even more special and wonderful for her.

Ruth was remarkable and so were the other women that came to be part of the Settlement House. Remember we called these women "teacher" and when you put their actions against the background of public schools, which was more judgmental and condemning about children of refugees, it was quite a difference. All this richness at the Center was in sharp contrast to what a nightmare the public schools were. For anyone in teaching, please, if you only do one thing for your students, do not write anyone off as impossible, even if you are tested to the fullest; no child is truly impossible.

Sometimes when I was acting my old self, bullying you know, at the Settlement and trying to make sure that everyone there was having a bad time, because I was in a bad mood or something, Miss Wright would not act mean to me or throw me out, she would tell me that I had to leave the room until I chose to have a good time. So, I would leave, but I was usually back in two minutes, ready to have a good time, because I did not want to miss anything that was going on. She taught me that change was a new beginning.

I became Ruth's shadow. I was where she was. I adored her. She was a tough disciplinarian, but I loved her. One time, when I had worn down her patience, she sent me to the hardware store for a left handed-hammer and some other items that didn't exist, just to get rid of me for a while. I went to two hardware stores seeking these items. I was told that I must be mistaken in my wants. I insisted that if Miss Ruth wanted it, there must be some. One of the merchants figured it out, and knowing both me and Ruth, detained me for awhile. He said that the shipment had not come in yet. When I finally got back to the Settlement, she hugged me.

On one occasion, there was an important group from the Home Missionary Society touring the Settlement. This was the group that gave most of the financial support that was needed for the program. Ruth asked Katie and me to serve the ladies at a special silver tea party. There were all kinds of fancy stuff, special cookies, small sandwiches, and most of the ladies arrived with pretty white gloves. Ruth tried to give Katie and me lessons on how to be proper servers. She told us when we served, we should be polite and say, "would you like a cookie", and never say "another cookie."

Well, these ladies really liked to eat, and Katie and I had to keep going to the kitchen to fill the trays. We were getting tired of running back and forth, so we began to say, "do you want another cookie, you've only had three or four." It was the first time I ever saw Ruth lose her patience; she pulled Katie and me into the kitchen and told us to straighten up and not to disappoint her.

Utica was a true melting pot with numerous first and second-generation immigrants. It was not unusual for hostilities to arise between the different ethnic pockets. Major streets in the city marked imaginary borders between rival gangs, and crossing those borders could result in fights and violence. Ruth wanted us to appreciate other cultures. She organized cultural awareness programs and we would make meals with different recipes from foreign countries. We would also dress up in costumes that looked like what people wore in those countries. Ruth felt that this would help us learn to understand the people in our city as well as young people from all over the world.

I was always organizing street baseball games or other activities, and I guess Ruth recognized that the traits that made me a bully could be nurtured and changed to make me a better leader. She worried about the lack of play space for children in the neighborhood. Kids were running in the road, and she feared their being struck by a car or hurt in some other way. She charged me with the task of building a playground for the children in the neighborhood on the vacant lot next to the building on Mary Street.

The playground was my first real opportunity to give back to the settlement. I agreed to do it, because I thought I could use some of those gambling games, like Bingo and raffles, which the Catholic Church did, to raise money. Miss Ruth said that I could not do anything that included gambling, because the Methodists would not support that. Even so, I was determined not to fail, I couldn't fail; I could not let Miss Ruth down. The Center had never failed me.

Since we had been involved with the cultural classes, having a festival to celebrate our heritage seemed like an ideal plan. Additionally, the religious festivals of my neighborhood were always successful. Committees were formed and many people contributed ideas. We had all kinds of people in the neighborhood. All were just as poor as the next family, but they were rich in pride. We spent the next few months planning the activity. We also worked on creating items that could be sold as part of the festival. We used our vocational classes to make stenciled and decorated towels and other fabric projects. We sold jewelry that we had made out of shells, and we made lots of useful articles that could be used in the home.

Music was made from the sound of hands popping air over the mouth, spoons tapping rhythm or harmonicas playing. More accomplished performing artists would play their instruments, sing or dance. All kinds of ethnic foods were brought to the Center for the festival, made by the women and then re-bought by their own families to take home again. Italian women would make big bowls of pasta and pizza fritte. The old men would lift their hands above their heads and do one of the simple dances from the old country and couples would dance.

The festival lasted for three nights, and we invited other ethnic groups, like the Polish and the Syrians, from around the community to participate. They were proud to let others see the heritage that they celebrated. Talk about a feeling of cultural diversity! Each night, an important city official or citizen opened the program. The festival raised $1,000 toward paving the cinder-covered lot to create a playground, furnishing it, and installing a wire fence to enclose it. The fence was to keep balls from going out into the street, not to keep kids out. We got used swings and chinning bars donated. In later years, the city loaned us its band shell for these festivals. The spotlights and stage attracted people from all over the community, as well as the neighborhood. The performing artists began to be better known. It became a real city-wide festival.

Ruth appointed me, at the age of sixteen, to be the Playground Director. Because of the popularity of the festival, three or four times during the summer I would open the playground area. Entire families would come to the settlement to enjoy the music playing and Italian songs, polkas and other entertainment. It was a good place for the entire family to go on Friday nights.

Under Ruth, the Italian Settlement's name was changed to the Neighborhood Center. She felt it reflected the diversity of the neighborhood better. She worked hard to get us to be part of the United Way program. With her interest in social work, she wanted the Center to reflect all the cultures that were now making up the neighborhood in the 1940's and 1950's. She really wanted to do a lot more with day care and child development. She was able to get skilled social workers and teachers into those positions. They would work with behavior and the development of the child, and the focus on the family. She wanted to see us take on more responsibility in citizenship and do more that would include adult group work.

When Ruth became the Director in 1945, her feeling was that the people who came to the settlement were already churched and that had their own religion. East Utica was predominately Christian, although there was also a large Jewish pocket in another part of the city. She did not try to convert the people who came to the

Settlement to be Methodists, as Miss Edick did. Ruth believed strongly in her faith and her denomination, but she was more social work orientated.

Ruth was part of the Home Missionary Society, but I don't think she was ever made a Deaconess. She modeled her Christian behavior and attitude. She helped mediate our behavior. She helped you see things that were good in the neighborhood and the family. Ruth helped you work out your problems and concerns as they related to school and life in general. She had a way of making you reach deep down inside yourself.

When I became 17, the Center became the central focus of my life. That is when I realized it would change my destiny. When I graduated high school and went to college, I continued to work at the Center during the summer and on school holidays. I earned about $200 a year.

When I graduated from Morningside College, I desperately wanted to live and work at the Center, but Ruth said there were no openings on the staff. Unknown to me at the time, and perhaps one of the most generous things my father ever did for me, he spoke with Ruth and told her that he would give her the money for my wages, if she would hire me. He knew how passionately I wanted to work there.

Ruth told him that it was not the wages, or the staffing that was the issue, but the education. She felt that I needed a master's degree. She finally agreed that I could intern and live at the Center for a year. The internship provided me the opportunity to be accepted into Columbia University's School of Social Work, where I earned my Master's Degree.

I came back full time in 1957, as an adult employee of the Center. The workers all lived at the Center then; we still did up until the 1980's when the living space was converted into much needed offices. The workers at the Settlement lived on the second floor. Some of the workers had to share a room, and everyone shared the living room and bathroom.

So, in 1957, I had gone out into the world, got my degrees, and ended up right smack back across the street from where I had grown up. I was home, and there was no place else on earth that I wanted to be. I wanted to make a difference, and give back to my community the love, compassion and support that had been given to me at the Settlement.

As I said, Ruth was an inspiration and a visionary. She initiated some projects that reached around the world. In one, we began to learn about the pain of rebuilding a war-torn country. We raised funds and were able to send the money to purchase 1000 chickens and goats to send overseas.

Through the Women's Division, we also made contact with the head of the Pestalozzi City School in Florence, Italy. We collected small toys, personal items, made beautiful puppets and sent five boxes of supplies to the school. I can remember Ruth not letting us get too comfortable or complacent with the jobs and tasks we were doing. Regardless of what we had just finished, our moment of self-basking in success was limited. Ruth would already be thinking about the next project and, with a smile, she would encourage us to push ourselves forward. "There's work to be done" she would say, and she was right; there always was something waiting to be tackled.

Ruth wanted me to work with the teens to create a conservation program to get the people in the neighborhood to take more pride in their property. We had lots of families by this time that would move in and out, the new ones always poorer than the ones that left. So I did. I took some of the neighborhood kids and we formed the Junior Citizen's for Community Improvement group in the summer.

We made a little map of our area. It covered about one fourth of a mile in all directions from our Mary Street location. We went up to Rutger Street, down to Catherine, over to Kossuth, and then to John Street. We carried with us tools and we worked to fix things that were broken. Sometimes, the sidewalk needed a little cement and we would haul a wheelbarrow and a scraper, or maybe there was a lot that needed to have the grass cut, or sometimes we would just sweep up the trash along the curb. Anything we could do to get the neighborhood to take more pride in its appearance.

As we walked around the neighborhood, we would carry a little clipboard, and use it to make a list of things that needed to be repaired and the bigger things we could not do. Like the houses that, you know, had broken windows, bad roofs, gardens that needed to be weeded, or planted whatever, and then we would leave or mail a note to the homeowner and tell them that we really wanted to work with them to help keep our neighborhood beautiful. We would help them if they would work with us on the repairs, even if they only planted a flowerpot or something. And you know, seeing those kids out there, those teenagers, raking, mowing, and all that stuff, seemed to start a transformation. People began to plant gardens, and rake their yard, or mow their lawns.

We made up little placards telling them how much the Center and the kids appreciated them helping to make the neighborhood better. And the kids kind of policed each other, too. No one had better trample down a flower planted by our group, or throw trash down or break a window. The word was out and the kids were policing the neighborhood. No fights or anything happened. It was just kind of known that these kids would be watching out for you. And, before this, they were probably the main ones breaking the windows and stuff.

Ruth Wright served as Executive Director until Multiple Sclerosis forced her retirement in 1967. Due to her declining health, I had been doing much of her work. When I accepted the position of Executive Director, Ruth continued to live at the

Center and I cared for her until her death. As I became older, and especially when I began to assume the caregiver role for Ruth as her MS progressed, I cherished the trips we made together to her vacation home.

Sewing class display

Boys' Basketball Recreation

Furniture made in the a Woodworking Class

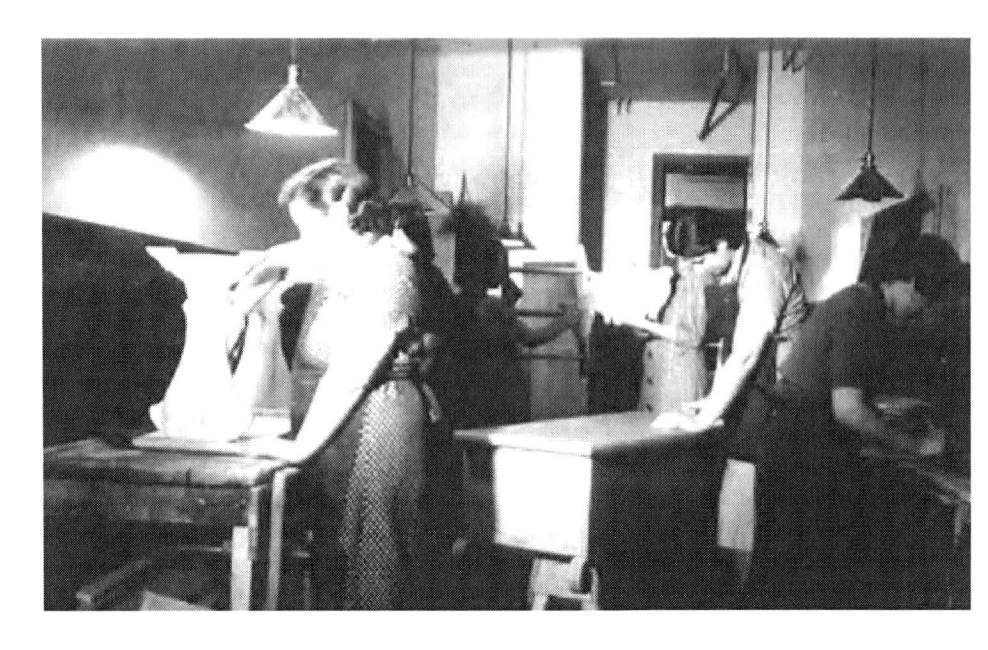

Furniture making class for women

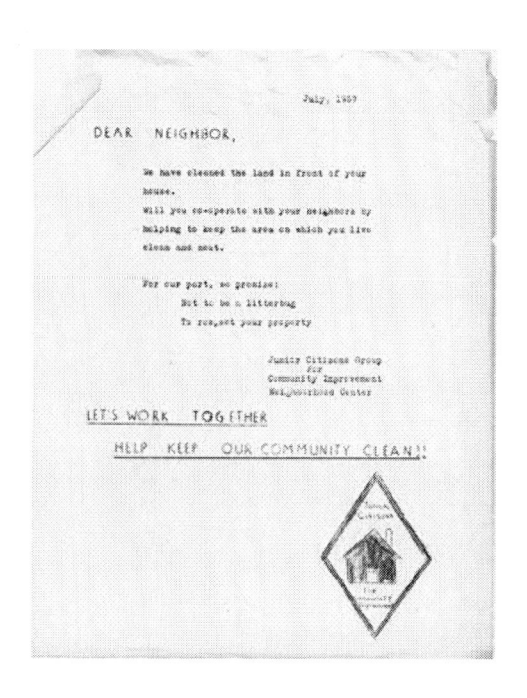

Notice given out by the Junior Citizens Group led by Marie

Women heading out to work as day labor on an area farm

Children participating in a Sunday School class

After school program

Marie (on left) participating in the Marionette Class

Marie (far left) at the Eagle, preparing for the New England Bike Trip

61

Marie (1st row – right end) with teen group on a trip to NYC

Cultural Awareness Activities sponsored by Miss Wright

Kindergarten Class

Backyard Garden

CHAPTER NINETEEN
NARRATIVE SIX: MARIE RUSSO'S PERCEPTION OF THE IMPORTANCE OF THE ITALIAN SETTLEMENT HOUSE

It taught me to dream, to be able to stand with pride and dignity. To boldly know that I was part of something meaningful, and it was, and is, something valuable enough that it, and its history, should be passed on into the whole entity that is the heritage of man.

There was something about the staff at the Center. Workers there simply and gently worked to change my behavior. The hostile, aggressive behaviors that I had when I was a child were necessary for survival back then. The women of the Settlement did not criticize or try to change us; they just tried to modify our behavior. They tried to give alternative ways in which we could learn some of those behaviors that were acceptable to society. For me, this really was like the beginning of the rest of my life.

These women were amazing, and even more, they came into the neighborhood to live with us. They saw the goodness, the richness, and the strengths of our world, and helped us to recognize them also. They pointed out the golden threads that were also a part of the fabric of ghetto life.

We use everything we have, gestures, words, touches, tears, everything, just to tell others that we are here, we are important. Sometimes we feel love, sometimes we feel hurt, we need, and we dream. There is no struggle greater than trying to let ourselves be known, and in the process find out who we are. It is so easy to create a label for someone and to accept those labels. How quickly a child can live up to the labels of being low-motivated, uninspired and deprived. It is so easy to believe that the welfare recipient is just a social parasite. It is easy for us to despise him.

Because of the Settlement House, we did not have to leave or reject our world. The teachers, the workers, and the missionaries helped us to see that the new was always within us. They heard not only what we said, but dared to hear what we left unsaid. The people of the Settlement House were people whose dreams were alive. They inspired dreams in our hearts, and minds, and they set about the task of helping us find ways in which our dreams could come true.

They showed us how to be strong, strong enough to use the gifts that God gave us. Thank God for the Women's Home Missionary Society and the Women's Division of the Methodist Church that founded and supported the Settlement House. It was a place where I could go and no one ridiculed me for having "foreign ways."

The women of the Settlement seemed to build you up. They gave you self-esteem. They gave you meaningful experiences. They were just so aware of our needs at a time in our lives when we could have gone much astray. I could feel valued and loved. This could not have been easy for the workers as I was not the kind of kid that was easy to love. So my self-esteem grew. I knew I was important to someone; I mattered.

I know all about Jane Addams and the Hull House. It is a great story, but ours is a great story, too. We did not have a big school like the University of Chicago helping us, we were a much smaller city, but our problems were just as big and just as real. Their story has been told a hundred times because of the college, but no one has ever taken the time to tell our story. Hull House now is listed as a National Historic Site and the University of Chicago has taken it over as a museum. We have a beautiful, historic building, but no support to save and preserve it. It is sinking. The foundation is slowly giving way to the culvert it was built upon. We need thousands of dollars to preserve the building that has been so important to East Utica.

Today, the people coming into the neighborhood we serve, are not unlike those who were part of my own personal history. Today, they are Hispanics, Bosnian, West Asians and other refugees; people looking for a chance to have a new start.

I don't regret not getting married or having children. I have had a lifetime love affair with the Neighborhood Center. And I have had thousands of kids and great success stories about my kids.

The Neighborhood Center is one of over seventy United Methodist supported community centers serving children in the United States. The Settlement taught us a sense of mission and responsibility to all things. We wanted to make progress and to be self-sufficient. We never had enough funds to provide what was needed. I spoke to many church groups to request funds, applied for all kinds of grants, and started the "Marie Russo Dream Fund."

During my tenure as Executive Director, the Center grew from a staff of five, with a budget of $60,000 to a staff of 200 serving more than 20,000 people a year with a budget in excess of $6,000,000. From the single building on Mary Street, the facilities of the Center have grown to include eleven buildings with programs in Utica and the City of Rome, NY.

The Settlement was where early intervention could heal and transform the lives of children who were broken by child abuse and neglect. The Settlement welcomed children who were socially and emotionally dysfunctional, children who were depressed, angry, and full of rage. I was one of those children. Because of the healing powers of the Settlement, I was able to have a future, free of judgment and the ability to grow and be realized.

Let me speak for those of us who are the beneficiaries of the settlement houses throughout the world. Their presence helped to realize the giant power within me and within my neighborhood. And with it came the freedom to discover and use more fully my, our, creative human resources to better serve the needs of people.

Summer fun from an outdoor shower on the playground

CHAPTER TWENTY
MY UTICA

I can't scribe Marie's story without weaving in parts of my own, for I too have an oral history of the Settlement to share and preserve. For both of us, the settlement provided the tools we needed to succeed.

Comparisons could be made with the early life of Marie and mine. We both grew up in the neighborhood that was part of the Center's service area, both came to the area through the relocation of our parents seeking new employment opportunities, and both enjoyed many positive experiences at the Neighborhood Center. While Marie and I might have walked the same walk, played in the same places, and navigated our own challenges of being urban poor, my family's poverty stemmed from the untimely death of my father, leaving my mother at the age of forty, a widow with five children to raise. Marie's poverty was rooted in discrimination, prejudice and social injustices.

My involvement with the Neighborhood Center was different than that of Marie's. For her, the Italian Settlement House was a refuge from horrific living conditions, cultural ridicule and educational failure. For me, the Center was a safe place for recreation. I entered the doors of the Center because of previous participation by my siblings and as an extension of the activities of my church. I chose to stay because value was found in the activities and the nurture that was so much a part of the Center's fabric. For me, one of the most valued aspects of the Center, and one that is shared by Miss Russo in her oral history, is that the staff of the Center went out into the neighborhood they served. It was one of the significant factors that separated the settlement house from other agencies in the community. Additionally, my mother was a member of the Board of Directors. At one time, four generations of my family participated in events there.

Unlike Miss Russo, parental support for me was evident in all aspects of my family life. Education was valued by my mother and family members. My siblings and I earned good grades, and positive reports issued by school personnel were expected at home. I had caring teachers and within my family there was never a question about going to college, the question was rather, which college I would attend. In addition to the

Center activities, I was involved with Scouting, church youth groups, and school clubs.

The Utica of my youth was different from Marie's. On the long hot summer days we would be awakened by the bells tolling the hour from St. John's. No one had air conditioners. We had noisy window fans that blew the hot humid air from outside around our bedrooms. With that air came the amazing fragrances of our neighborhood. Like the incredible aroma of fresh bread baking from the Wonder Bread plant four blocks from our house. If you went on their tour, they would give you a tiny loaf of bread to take with you. Thirty Wonder Bread wrappers and a dime would get you into the Saturday matinee at the Olympic Theater.

During my youth, the population of the city was over 100,000 and our schools were integrated. JFK's immortal words of asking what we could do for our nation, and service organizations like the Peace Corp all created a new social consciousness that began to tilt the scales more and more towards equality. Some of the Neighborhood Center staff members were part of the volunteer "US2" mission program of the Methodist Church. Much like the original workers of the settlement programs, these staff members came from throughout the country to work and live at the Center for two or more years. Some of those missionaries would attend the Sunday services at my church, Central Methodist. Our church often displayed information about the Center and its programs. The women's group and the youth group would raise funds and collect materials and supplies for the Center.

I attended Bleecker Street School. We were not bused. Children stayed in their own neighborhood and walked to the schools. The school had two entrances, one for the boys and one for the girls. We were never allowed to play together on the playground during recess. The bathrooms were located in the basement of the building, and from time to time a bat or two would escape from the old bell tower causing our teachers with their stiffly teased and sprayed hair to scurry we children to another part of the building. We had no cafeteria. We had a midday break and we all walked to our homes for lunch. Sometimes my mother, who worked as the school crossing guard, would stop and pick up a slice or two of pizza from one of the many corner pizzerias.

My mother never missed a P.T.A. meeting, and for many years served as an officer for the organization. I can remember the amazing bake sales the PTA would hold during the school year. Cupcakes dripping with frosting could be purchased for a nickel and cookies were two cents.

One of our high school teachers, Mr. DeVito, who we all loved, sponsored the Italian Club. Though I did not take his class, I was somehow elected to be secretary of the club and on special outings he would take us to the bakery his father had started, and his brother now operated. It was around the corner from the Center. One afternoon when the bakery was closed, he took our entire club over and showed us how to roll out the dough and make savory sweet sausage bread. As we rolled the dough he shared some of his memories of growing up in the neighborhood and times he had spent at the Center.

In defining the neighborhood and the ethnic and social surroundings, it would be easiest to think in terms of the main streets and the block portions between those streets. Genesee Street was the main business hub. The Boston Store, Woolworth's, trendy boutiques and expensive dress shops lined the street. The Utica Public Library on Genesee Street remains an impressive building. It had a tremendous collection of books, and the Children's Room was always welcoming. I loved the story hour, the wooden tables, the carpet on the floor and the long rows of books. One section of the library had glass floors. The main offices of the Neighborhood Center are now located on Genesee Street.

Bleecker Street was a main area of commerce for the Italian population in Utica. Three blocks below Bleecker, was the train station, which had been built primarily by Italian laborers. John Street had little shops, apartment buildings, a funeral home, and St John's Catholic Church. It was more a commercial street than residential.

The homes between John and First grew from the early railroad and downtown businesses. There were a large number of apartment houses on Elizabeth Street. Mary Street mixed in a few single family homes and Blandina boasted of lovely Victorian styled residences or two-family homes. These Victorians once were the homes of railroad officials, local judges, politicians and the new middle class.

When built, the wealthy and the elite lived in the sprawling homes on Rutger Street. They were considered to be mansions and had well manicured lawns and large gardens. Most were fenced and had gated driveways. Mansions also dotted Genesee Street. Vice President James Schoolcraft Sherman, who served with Taft, had been Utica's mayor, and had lived in one of the beautiful homes. By the 60's, the Syrians dominated most of the businesses on John Street. Many of the apartment houses were owned by absentee landlords, and the upper middle class had abandoned Rutger Street for the suburbs. The houses in the area had started to decay

Crossing First Street was like entering a new neighborhood. As travelers headed toward Mohawk Street, more and more homes with statues of the Virgin Mary in their windows or small front gardens could be found. Half English, half Italian phrases could be heard from the doorways. The aroma of freshly fried fish would seep through the neighborhood as Catholics upheld the tradition of no meat on Friday. On the other side of Mohawk Street, was the Ukrainian Orthodox Church. On Saturdays, the women of the church boiled pierogi and made Babka Bread.

With friends and family we would eat pizza at Pescatore's at the corner of Albany and Blandina Street. The aromas filled the neighborhood, especially when Frankie Nash was cooking. Pellettieri Joe's on Jay Street was also a family favorite. They served fresh soft Italian bread, but we could not ask for butter. To do so would result in some rude retort from the waiter and our being informed that we needed to eat our bread with the freshly grated Parmesan cheese delivered to our table in a small saucer with a spoon. I loved their fried peppers, dripping with the sweet flavors of olive oil, freshly ground herbs and spices. Their house specialty, mushroom strew, piled high on pasta, was to die for.

We would purchase half moon cookies at Hemstrought's Bakery. and fresh ricotta cannolis at Caruso's. Chanatry's on Culver Ave was known for their fresh meats. The Florentine Bakery made an incredible rum cake with a sweet cream filling. Rosato's Bakery had chocolate iced cookies and tomato pie with individual slices wrapped in wax paper bags. The Star Bakery, Jean's Beans and the fresh fish markets like the one on Kossuth Ave were all part of my Utica.

My favorite, and one that I still go to when I go back to Utica to visit family, was O'Scugnizzo Pizzeria on Bleecker near Third Avenue. A small cheese pizza sold for seventy-five cents and had six slices. We use to call it the "upside down" pizza, because the cheese and all the toppings lay under the sauce.

CHAPTER TWENTY-ONE
MY CENTER

My physical image of the Center was an impressive brick structure. The original entrance was an open stairway however, when I attended, it had been enclosed and covered to protect participants from the extreme weather conditions that are common to upstate New York.

Heavy doors at the street level opened up to expose surface treated cement steps that ascended upward to the doors of the agency. The acoustics in the room made a marvelous echo and we often sang a long note or recited a simple rhyme, just to hear our voices vibrate from the walls. On either side of the steps were long wooden planks. To prevent children from sliding down them and crashing on the cement flooring, diagonal pieces of wood framing had been attached in a repeating pattern down the slope of the planks.

At the top of the steps were the large tiled initials "WHMS" which stood for the Women's Home Missionary Society of the Methodist Church, the driving force behind the origins of the Settlement. This reference is most likely lost to the average visitor who might not have historical knowledge of the settlement.

There were adult activities for the neighborhood ladies during the day and in the evening. There was also a full day nursery school. For my friends and me, our programs would begin at 3:45. The programs at the Center were very structured and if we arrived early, we had to stay in this hallway until the glass and wood doors that separated the entrance from the classrooms were unlocked. I can still recall the cold tile on my skirt covered bare legs as I sat on the top step amusing myself with the echoes or tracing the WHMS letters with my fingers.

The main floor of the settlement had classrooms and a kitchen that was used for cooking classes. Home Economic type programs like cooking and sewing for girls, and shop like programs for boys were part of the regular programming. During the day, the same kitchen was used to prepare meals for the nursery children. Before the start of every class we would have a snack of cold milk and sliced cheese. It was part of a government surplus program, but we did not know it then.

Many of the windows in the facility were decorated with stained glass. A brass plaque beneath them identified patrons who donated funds for the building. Steps led downstairs to the basement area where a large meeting room and a small stage were located. At one time the room had been a small gymnasium.

At the end of the hall was a bathroom with a single toilet and pedestal sink. There was a large drain in the middle of the floor and we were told that many years' earlier people in the neighborhood would come there to take a bath. Naturally that would create a chorus of giggles and laughter from a generation of city children who had no concept of cold water flats and outhouses. The bathroom also served as the dressing room for the girls when our drama club presented little skits or the Christmas pageant was performed on the tiny wooden stage. The girl's choir used it to get ready in when they preformed a small program for the neighborhood adults and Center Board members.

Facing the Mary Street building, the lot on the left contained a well maintained playground area. In the summer, we would enjoy the swings, jungle gym, see-saw, and paved areas. Boundaries for games of softball, basketball, and square ball had been painted on the pavement. There was a grassy area for small group play, a sandbox and a craft area. From the basement, there was an entrance to the playground through the boiler room. Most times we were not allowed in that part of the building unless an unexpected lightening storm descended upon the playground and the staff wanted to quickly bring us inside for safety. We were also not allowed to go up to the third floor of the building, for that was the living quarter for the settlement workers.

On really hot summer days, the Center staff would open up a large shower like head from the side of the building. We would take turns running through the cooling spray. The Center would also take us to the YWCA where Center staff members gave us swimming lessons as part of their summer program. The Bowling Club met off site at a nearby alley.

The Center held an Arts Festival in the summer. The city gave us the large band shelter to use. Local groups would perform and politicians would speak. It was quite an event!. Many of the Italian women of the neighborhood would volunteer their time to make and sell pastries and pizza fritta, lightly sprinkled with confectionary sugar. The Center's festival celebrated the cultural diversity of the neighborhood, without a religious theme, unlike the summer feasts and festivals at St Anthony's, St Anges and Mount Carmel. Old Italian men would sing songs and challenge the younger generation to games of bocce.

I want to be a role model to my children. I want to teach them to advocate for themselves. I want them to set goals and believe in their own worth and capabilities. I want them to stretch themselves and to become passionate and take a stand for what they believe. I want them to reach whatever height they can, without losing sight of who they are and where they came from.

Marie and all the individuals that touched and shaped the Neighborhood Center helped to instill those values within me. As a child of the Center, Marie knew and understood the struggles we had. She came from the same place we came from, went through, and surpassed the same kinds of challenges our neighborhood harbored, and taught us to navigate the same waters.

In me and through me flows the strength and wisdom of the women of my neighborhood. Be they the saintly figures where so many prayers were lifted up to them in the grotto of St. John's. Be they the women of faith who had a vision and built a settlement to meet the needs of the immigrants that came to my city. Be they the women who dedicated decades of their lives, and continue to do so, to keep that vision alive and bring opportunity for thousands like me. Be they the single mothers that struggle and sacrifice for the benefit of their children. *In me and through me* lies the opportunity to be a testament to their legacy and to offer to you, the opportunity to add your own story to the legacy.

BE THE LEGACY

Your support for the Neighborhood Center, Inc can be made through:

Neighborhood Center, Inc.
293 Genesee Street
Utica, New York 13501
Read more: http://neighborhoodctr.org/home0.aspx

Marie A. Russo Neighborhood Center Institute, Inc
c/o Daniel L. Clark
293 Genesee Street
Utica, NY 13501
Read more: http://www.faqs.org/tax-exempt/NY/Marie-A-Russo-Neighborhood-Center-Institute-Inc.html#ixzz2BGPY3Fr3

United Methodist Women
National Ministries
NMI - Neighborhood Center, Inc
Project 3019239

http://secure.gbgm-umc.org/donations/umw/donate.cfm?code=3019239&dg=Neighborhood+Center++Inc.%2C+Utica%2C+NY&div=3&donate=Donate+To+This+NMI+Project

The author invites you to be part of:

"The House On Mary Street – Our Story"

A collection of memories about individual experiences with the Neighborhood Center.

If you would like to share your oral history of how the Neighborhood Center enriched your life, or the *in you - through you* gifts you have given to the Center, please contact the author.

Anticipated publication date: November, 2014
Oral History Due Date: August 1, 2014
Oral histories for this publication may be limited, so as to provide a collection that offers depth and variety as "our stories" unfold.

Information to include:

- Full name
- Contact information (address, phone, e-mail, etc)
- Relationship with the Center (participant, staff, board member, community support, church support, etc)
- The years (length of time and dates) you were affiliated with the Center (i.e. 1945 – 1957; 2007 – 2012)
- Scanned black and white photographs are welcome. Please identify the event and participants in the photo. (A release may be required prior to publication)
- The history or story that you would like to share. Please submit using Microsoft WORD or a compatible format, double spaced, 12 Font.

Submit to Dr. Kathryn H. Beard at:
thehouseonmarystreet@yahoo.com

RESOURCES

Axinn, J. & Levin, H. (1997). *Social welfare: a history of the American response to need.* White Plains, NY: Longman.

Bakey, D., Gee, M., Kramer, C., & Varano, D. (1976). *Program Analysis of Service Systems Conciliation Report of The Assessment of The Neighborhood Center.* SUNY at Utica/Rome, NY: Public Service Department of Upper Division College.

Barbuto, D. (1999). *American settlement houses and progressive social reform.* Phoenix, AZ: The Oryx Press.

Beard, K.H. (2010). *Marie Russo: An Oral History of the Italian Settlement House.* Charlottesville, VA. University of Virginia Press

Buck, S. (2006) *A brief history of the international order of the King's Daughters and Sons.* Retrieved from: http://www.iokds.org/history.html

Carson, M. (1990). *Settlement folk: social thought and the American settlement movement, 1885 – 1930.* Chicago, IL: University of Chicago Press.

Crisafulli, V. (1977). Agriculture. *The history of Oneida County.* Utica, NY: C. L. Hutson Co.,Inc. 49 – 52.

Ernst, R. (1965). *Immigrant life in New York City.* Port Washington, NY: Ira J. Friedman, Inc.

Evans, S. (1998, May 6). Marie Russo of the Neighborhood Center: "To Have A Dream is to Have a Possibility." *Boonville Herald,* Boonville, NY. p. 22.

Glazer, N. & Moynihan, D. (1970). *Beyond the melting pot: the Negroes, Puerto Ricans, Jews, Italians and Irish of New York City.* 2nd Ed. Cambridge, MA: The M.I.T. Press.

Gordon, H. (2008). *The history and growth of career and technical education in America* (3rd ed.). Prospect Heights, IL: Waveland Press.

Italian Settlement House. (1933). *Annual Report.* Utica, NY : Edick, H.

Lannie, V. (1967). The development of vocational education in America: An historical overview. In C. J. Schaefer & J. J. Kaufman (Eds.) *Vocational education: A prospectus for change.* Boston, MA: Massachusetts Advisory Council on Education.

Lee, A. (1969). Young Londoner Comes To Utica. *Response Magazine. 1*(9).

Lynch, J. (2005). *The Facts of Reconstruction.* (New York: 1913) An e-book retrieved from: http://www.gutenberg.org/files/16158/16158-h/16158-h.htm

Maurizio, F. (1980 June, 30). Youth Center Dedicated to Give A Child a Dream. *The Daily Press, p. 9.*

Mazza, Salvatore B. 1967. *Ruth Wright Recognition Day.* Neighborhood Center of Utica, NY. Program Book. Utica, NY

Meeker, R. E. 1969. *Six Decades of Service. 1880 - 1940 A History of the Women's Home Missionary Society of The Methodist Episcopal Church.* Syracuse, NY: Central New York Conference of the United Methodist Church. 231-233.

.National Association of Social Workers. (2003a). *Professional Development Workshop:.* Revitalize your Skills. Reconnect with your Peers. Renew your Energy. Rochester, NY: NASW.

National Association of Social Workers. (2003b) *The Spirit of Social Work.* Washington, DC: NASW. Street, C.

Neighborhood Center. (1952, June 29). *Annual Meeting.* The Director Reports. Utica, NY: Wright, R.

Neighborhood Center. (1966, May 31). *Annual Meeting.* A Message From The Executive. Change Is A New Beginning. Utica, NY:Wright, R. p.7.

Neighborhood Center, Inc. (1957, July). Flyer. *Dear Neighbor*. Junior Citizens Group.

Neighborhood Center of Utica, Inc. (1976). 1976 *Annual Report*. Neighborhood Center – an experience in human development. The future is now. Mazza, S.

Neighborhood Center of Utica, NY, Inc. (1980). *1979-1980 Annual Report*. Chairman's Message. Old and New Dreams. Frey, C.

Neighborhood Center of Utica, NY, Inc. (2000). *Annual Report*. Russo, M.

Neighborhood Center, Inc. (2009). Retrieved from: http://www.charityadvantage.com/theneighborhoodcentercny/NeighborhoodCenterHome.asp

Nettleship, L. (1982). William Fremantle, Samuel Barnett and the Broad Church Origins of Toynbee Hall. *Journal of Ecclesiastical History. 51* (4) 366-461.

Northern New York Conference Methodist Episcopal Church. (1905). Thirty-Third Annual Session . *Annual Report*. Official Minutes. Published by the Secretaries of the NNYC MEP. Watertown, NY: Hungerford-Holbrook Co.: Hamond, J.

Northern New York Conference Methodist Episcopal Church. (1906). Thirty-Fourth Annual Session . *Annual Report*. Official Minutes. Published by the Secretaries of the NNYC MEP. Watertown, NY: Hungerford-Holbrook Co.: Hamond, J.

Northern New York Conference Methodist Episcopal Church. (1907). Thirty-Fifth Annual Session . *Annual Report*. Official Minutes. Published by the Secretaries of the NNYC MEP. Watertown, NY: Hungerford-Holbrook Co.: Hamond, J.

Northern New York Conference Methodist Episcopal Church. (1908). Thirty-Sixth Annual Session . *Annual Report*. . Official Minutes. First Methodist Episcopal Church. Camden, NY. Published by the Secretaries of the NNYC MEP. Watertown, NY: Hungerford-Holbrook Co.: Shepard, E. L. 60 -79.

Northern New York Conference Methodist Episcopal Church. (1909). Thirty-Seventh Annual Session . *Annual Report*. Official Minutes. Published by the Secretaries of the NNYC MEP. Watertown, NY: Hungerford-Holbrook Co.: Hamond, J.

Northern New York Conference Methodist Episcopal Church. (1910). Thirty-Eighth Annual Session . *Annual Report*. Official Minutes. Published by the Secretaries of the NNYC MEP. Watertown, NY: Hungerford-Holbrook Co.: Hamond, J.

Northern New York Conference Methodist Episcopal Church. (1911). Thirty-Ninth Annual Session . *Annual Report*. Official Minutes. Published by the Secretaries of the NNYC MEP. Watertown, NY: Hungerford-Holbrook Co.: Hamond, J.

Northern New York Conference of the Methodist Episcopal Church. (1912) Fortieth Annual Session . *Annual Report*. Official Minutes. Published by the Secretaries of the NNYC MEP. Work Among The Italians In Utica and Vicinity. Watertown, NY: Hungerford-Holbrook Co. Hammond, J., Caldwell, W., & Walton, C. pg 74-76

Northern New York Conference of the Methodist Episcopal Church (1924, October, 24). *Annual Report: A Valedictory Statement*. Women's Home Missionary Society. Hunt, A.

One Way To Beat High Prices of Hats. (1952, n.d.). *Observer Dispatch*. Utica, NY p.1

Preston, D, & Ellis D. (1977). The Ethnic Dimension. In Oneida County Bicentennial Committee (Eds.) *The history of Oneida County*. Utica, NY: C. L. Hutson Co., Inc. (pg 59 -66).

Price, B. (1952, n.d.). Lines on Local Daughters. *Observer Dispatch*. Utica, NY.

Pula, J. (Ed.). (2005). *Ethnic Utica*. Syracuse, NY: Syracuse University Press.

Puppets Hailed By Italian Tots. (1952, n.d.). *Observer Dispatch*. Utica, NY

Schiro, G., (1975). *Americans by choice: history of the Italians in Utica*. New York, NY: Arno Press.

Schlesinger, A. (1957) *The Age of Roosevelt: The Crisis of the Old Order, 1919-1933*. Boston, MA: Houghton Mifflin.

She'll Study At Center. (1952, n.d.). *Observer Dispatch*. Utica, NY.

Taibi, J. (2003). *Rails along the Oriskany: a history of the New York, Ontario & Western railway's Utica division and Rome branch*. New York, NY: Purple Mountain Press.

They Get Our Goat. (1952, n.d.). *Observer Dispatch*. Utica, NY.

Virginia Cooperative Extension. (2004). *Extension Mission, Vision, History and Legislation*. Retrieved from: http://www.ext.vt.edu/about.vce/miss.html

Williams, S. (1980, June 29). It Was A Night Of Sharing for the 150 At Center's 75th Anniversary Program. *The Observer Dispatch*. Section C. p. 1.

Wright, R. (1948). A Community Helps Secure A Playground. *Urban News*. Second Quarter. Bureau of Urban Work. Women's Division of Christian Service. New York: NY. pp. 1 – 2.